DATE			
AUG 5 1991			
NOV 05 '91			

The Unconscious before Freud

Lancelot Law Whyte

Introduced by Arthur Koestler

Julian Friedmann Publishers London
St Martin's Press New York

This edition first published in 1978

In the United Kingdom by Julian Friedmann Publishers Ltd,
4 Perrins Lane, London, NW3 1QY

In the United States of America by St. Martin's Press, Inc.,
175 Fifth Avenue, New York, NY 10010

Text © E. Whyte 1978

Introduction © A. Koestler 1978

United Kingdom ISBN 0 904014 41 x
United States ISBN 0-312-82870-5

Library of Congress Catalog Card Number 78-61469

Introduction typeset by T & R Filmsetters
Printed and Bound by A. Wheaton & Co, Ltd, Exeter, England

Introduction

by Arthur Koestler

'I do not know of any more important book by a living writer,'
wrote Dame Edith Sitwell in her Foreword to the first edition of
The Unconscious Before Freud: 'It is enthralling for a poet . . .' In a
more restrained voice the *British Journal of Psychology* joined in the
praise: 'His [Whyte's] book should serve to wake at least some
psychologists from their dogmatic slumbering, and give them a
larger view of the subject matter of psychology.' It does not
happen often that a book receives such joint accolades, from a
poet of fastidious tastes and from a learned scientific journal.

One of the lasting merits of Whyte's book is its thorough
refutation of the popular belief that the concept of the
unconscious mind was, like Relativity or Quantum Physics, an
invention of the twentieth century. The 'Freudian Unconscious',
as it came to be eponymously known, acquired a clinical odour to
which, later on, Jung added a mystical halo. The 'Id' could be
regarded as a kind of Pandora's box, inhabited by demons of

various breeds, while the sceptical behaviourists asserted that it was empty.

However, the concept of the unconscious mind was no more invented by Freud than evolution was invented by Darwin, and it has an equally distinguished ancestry which can be traced back to antiquity. Whyte – very wisely, I think – refrains from burdening his readers with obscure quotations from the *Upanishads* or ancient Egypt, and starts his history of the unconscious with the dawn of Christian Europe, when the dominant influence on philosophy were the Neoplatonists, foremost among them Plotinus, who apparently took it for granted that 'feelings can be present without our being aware of them', and that 'the absence of conscious perception is no proof of the absence of "mental activity".' He also produced a striking metaphor: there is a 'mirror' in the mind which, when correctly aimed, reflects the processes going on inside that mind, and when displaced or broken fails to do so – yet the processes continue all the same, and 'thus thought is present without an inner image of itself'.

St Augustine, too, marvelled at man's immense store of unconscious memories and its 'limitless depth'. In fact, the knowledge of unconscious mentation had always been there – as Whyte shows with an abundance of quotations from theologians like St Thomas Aquinas, mystics like Jacob Boehme or St John of the Cross, physicians like Paracelsus, astronomers like Kepler, writers and poets as far apart as Dante, Cervantes, Shakespeare and Montaigne. Yet this shared, fundamental insight into the working of the human mind was lost under the impact of the scientific revolution, and more particularly of its most influential philosopher, René Descartes.

As modern cosmology started with the Newtonian revolution, so modern philosophy starts with what one might call the Cartesian catastrophe. The catastrophe consisted not so much in the splitting up of the world into the realms of matter and mind (more sophisticated versions of dualism are still arguable today), but in the *identification of 'mind' with conscious thinking*. The result of this fallacious identification was the shallow rationalism of *l'esprit Cartesien,* and an impoverishment of psychology which it took three centuries to remedy even in part. But the Cartesian catastrophe had a further unexpected consequence, which Whyte describes in a key passage of this book (italics in the original):

'Prior to Descartes and his sharp definition of the dualism there was no cause to contemplate the possible existence of unconscious mentality as part of a separate realm of mind. Many religious and speculative thinkers had taken for granted factors lying outside but influencing immediate awareness . . . Until an attempt had been made (with apparent success) to choose *awareness* as the defining characteristic of an independent mode of being called mind, there was no occasion to invent the idea of unconscious mind as a provisional correction of that choice. It is only after Descartes that we find, first the idea and then the term, "unconscious mind" entering European thought.'

From the end of the seventeenth century onward, the idea gradually spread among the pioneers who came to realise that 'if there are two realms, physical and mental, awareness cannot be taken as the criterion of mentality (because) the springs of human nature lie in the unconscious, as the realm which links the moments of human awareness with the background of organic processes within which they emerge.'

In other words, since Cartesian philosophy had no room for it, the concept of the unconscious had to be re-invented. Before Descartes it had been taken for granted; after its resurrection it became an object of intensive study. The leading figures in this new field were mostly to be found in England and Germany. As early as 1678 the English Platonist John Norris declared boldly:

'We may have ideas of which we are not conscious', and two centuries later, at the end of a chain of eminent scholars, Henry Maudsley wrote in his classic *Physiology and Pathology of the Mind*: 'The most important part of mental action, the essential process on which thinking depends, is unconscious mental activity.' In Germany there was an equally distinguished line of writers, from Goethe to Nietzsche, and of scholars, from Leibnitz to Fechner, a pioneer of experimental psychology, who coined the famous metaphor of the mind as an iceberg, with only a fraction of it above the surface of consciousness, moved by the winds of awareness, but mostly by hidden under-water currents. At about the same time (1868) Erich von Hartmann published his *Philosophy of the Unconscious* which became a bestseller. Whyte lists six philosophical works published within ten years after von Hartmann's, which carry the word 'unconscious' in their titles. He concludes (italics in the original):

'The general conception of unconscious mental process was *conceivable* (in post-Cartesian Europe) around 1700, *topical* around 1800, and *fashionable* around 1870-1880 . . . It cannot be disputed that by 1870-1880 the general conception of the unconscious mind was a European commonplace and that many special applications of this general idea had been vigorously discussed for several decades.'

Whyte's intent was not to belittle the greatness and originality of Freud – that would have been as silly as trying to run down Newton because he had 'stood on the shoulders of giants'. But while Newton was aware of this – the metaphor is his own – Freud, curiously, was not. He never realised how ancient and respectable the idea was on which he built his edifice.

*   *   *

The Unconscious Before Freud is a remarkable contribution to that much neglected branch of historiography, the History of Ideas. It is a short book, but I believe that it will take its place among such classics as Herbert Butterfield's *The Origins of Modern Science* and Lovejoy's *The Great Chain of Being*.

Lance Whyte started his career – or intellectual Odyssey – as a physicist working under Rutherford in Cambridge. His two earliest books – *Archimedes, or the Future of Physics* and *Critique of Physics* – created a stir because they attacked the philosophical assumptions underlying modern science. From physics he turned to biology and published a series of unorthodox but scholarly and well-documented books which turned him into a minor cult-figure among scientists discontented with the prevailing reductionist *Zeitgeist*. In spite of his heretical views, he was elected Chairman of the Philosophy of Science group of the British Society for the History of Science and held office from 1953 to 1955; he also lectured at various American universities and was a Fellow of the Centre for Advanced Study at Stanford and other 'Think Tanks'. He possessed great charm, equalled only by his insatiable intellectual appetite. I cannot think of a more fitting epitaph than Professor Whitrow's concuding lines in his obituary notice for Whyte in the *British Journal for the Philosophy of Science*:

'Although it is too soon to say which of Lancelot Whyte's many ideas will bear fruit, the catholicity of his interests and the unorthodoxy of his views, coupled with his infectious enthusiasm, acted as an intellectual stimulus. He was a fascinating talker and had an unrivalled gift for bringing together people with similar interests who, but for him, would probably never have met. Many of us owe him a great debt for encouraging us to look at old problems in a new way.'

London, June 1978

Foreword

In this "siècle à mains" there are yet adventurers who seek to conquer the universe, though the growth of the spirit from darkness is sometimes forgotten.

To read any work by Mr. Whyte, one of the most important thinkers and writers of our time, is an adventure comparable to those of Christopher Columbus and of Major Gagarin. These works seek to conquer the universe—are voyages of discovery but they deal also with the growth of the spirit.

* * *

The book of which I write is so vitalizing that after the long period of spiritual and mental darkness which comes to the artist after the completion of a work, I felt like a dying person when placed in an oxygen tent.

It is enthralling for a poet—(Mr. Whyte's works are amongst the most potent influences in *this* poet's life as an artist)— enthralling because it takes us through "the twilight realms of consciousness" which are the antecedents of "the morning redness"—the beginning of inspiration:

"When the flash is caught in the fountain of the heart" wrote Jacob Boehme, "then the Holy Ghost riseth up in the seven qualifying or fountain spirits into the brain, like the day-break, dawning of the day, or morning redness."

But a fruitful darkness comes before this experience. That fruitful night, and that morning redness we find in this book. I do not know of any more important book by a living writer. It is indeed a history of the development of Man.

EDITH SITWELL

Preface

The origins of this work lie back in the years
after the first World War, when psychoanalysis was a novelty
and I innocently imagined that Freud had just discovered the
unconscious mind. None of my teachers had explained to me
that major achievements are usually the culmination of a
cultural process extending over centuries.

So when I found that Nietzsche had expressed several of
the insights of Freud's doctrine twenty or more years before
him, I was greatly excited and could not understand why
neither Freud nor his interpreters had mentioned this significant fact. For such anticipations showed that the unconscious
mind was not just an invention of Freud's, but a step in the
discovery of objective truth, a necessary way of interpreting
the facts found independently by very different minds: an
intuitive philosopher and a clinical scientist.

This excitement has survived more than thirty years and
another World War, though my notes on those whom I then
regarded as Freud's predecessors have frequently been lost.

But my perspective has changed. It is now the state of European thought during the two hundred years before Freud that interests me. Moreover the early thinkers are not "predecessors" who "anticipated" Freud. They, and Freud, and countless others are participants in a tradition which is being slowly enriched. They did not "lead to Freud," for some of them knew much that Freud, rightly for his own purposes, preferred not to emphasize. Hence one way of improving current ideas is to recall what was thought and said in earlier times. The aim is not to project our ideas into the past, or to dazzle ourselves with the prescience of early thinkers as wise as we are, but to recognize where they knew more.

Thus what began as an interest in the "history of the idea of the unconscious before Freud" has become a study in the development of human awareness and of ideas: how the European individual first became intensely aware of his own faculty of consciousness, and then balanced this by also becoming aware *by inference* of much in his own mental processes of which he is not directly conscious. Freud is not final; he is the most influential figure in a succession of thinkers, all recognizing aspects of the truth. And Freud himself may be the anticipator of a more balanced doctrine that still lies out of sight.

The continuity of the tradition of human thought and the productive imagination of individuals are inseparable features of a single story. The individuals and the tradition mold each other. Thus Freud's greatness implies that he can only be adequately interpreted against several centuries of European thought.

When Volume I of Ernest Jones's biography of Freud appeared in 1953, and I found that he explained Freud's theory of the mind, not in the context of the development of European thought but in terms of academic and clinical psychology over the preceding fifty years, I was shocked into action. As

a start I gave a brief survey [1] of "the unconscious before
Freud" on the Third Programme of the B.B.C., calling attention to the ideas of Schelling, Carus, Schopenhauer, von Hartmann, and others.

At first I hesitated to attempt a more extensive study, regarding this as a task for a professional psychologist, philosopher, or historian. Then gradually, as the result of the response of audiences in Great Britain and the United States, I
came to realize that my interest in the matter was partly due
to a conviction, until then barely conscious, that historical
understanding can throw light on current problems. Thus a
study of the idea of the unconscious over the two hundred
years before Freud can, I believe, throw some light on the
limitations of contemporary ideas. This may be called *therapeutic history:* history revealing where current ideas are partial, the expression of transitory preoccupations and inhibitions. One can be fascinated by the past for its own sake, and
at the same time allow history to enlighten one. For past
thinkers, in their different contexts, knew much that we have
either forgotten or have not yet learned to express in mid-
twentieth-century language. Thus I came to feel that here
was a task appropriate to my situation and interests.

This book may perhaps be regarded as a contribution
toward the general education of the second half century, with
the twofold aim of using the historical approach to clarify and
unify foundations, and of warning the young from accepting
any one doctrine as absolute. The specialization of contemporary thought can be remedied by remembering our roots.

The hurried reader may welcome a summary of my main
assumptions and conclusions:

1. Ideas often come suddenly to individuals, but they usually have a long history.

2. There is seldom a monopoly in great ideas. The general
conception of unconscious mental processes, in a different

context, is implicit in many ancient traditions. The development of the idea in Europe—prior to the relatively precise theories of our time—occupied some two centuries, say 1680–1880, and was the work of many countries and schools of thought. The idea was forced on them as a response to facts; it was necessary to correct an overemphasis, c. 1600–1700, on the consciousness of the individual.

3. Criticism is the due of genius. Freud's greatness and lasting influence are here taken for granted. But his originality was *in some respects* less than he and others have imagined. Every generation exaggerates the achievements of the heroes it has created. The worthy followers of great men are those who seek to lessen any damage they may have done by showing where their ideas were inadequate or mistaken. In the case of Freud this task may take another half century.

4. For Freud to achieve what he did between 1895 and 1920 two conditions were necessary: that a long preparation should already have taken place and that he should himself be largely unaware of it, so that while unconsciously influenced by it he was free to make his own inferences from clinical observations.

5. The antithesis *conscious/unconscious* probably does *not* hold the clue to the further advance of psychological theory. It requires modification or reinterpretation in terms of more comprehensive and precise ideas. Some suggestions are made regarding these.

6. Reason has not yet learned what its precise limitations are, and none of the various sciences understands its own foundations. The application of supposedly scientific ideas and methods to the interpretation (let alone the control!) of human situations calls for the greatest caution. For example, this entire book should be set in giant quotation marks implying: "These concepts and assertions are all partial, being

borrowed from a tradition known to be inadequate, but they
are the best I can do now."

I wish to thank the countless friends, too numerous to cite,
who have helped with suggestions, making Chapters V–VIII
a collective product. Also my wife, Eve, for her invaluable
aid. Finally, the work would have been more difficult without the facilities of the Widener Library at Harvard, which
I enjoyed while holding a Graham Foundation Fellowship
(1958/59).

London, March 1960   **L. L. W.**

Contents

No one can take from us the joy of the first becoming aware of something, the so-called discovery. But if we also demand the honor, it can be utterly spoiled for us, for we are usually not the first.

What does discovery mean, and who can say that he has discovered this or that? After all it's pure idiocy to brag about priority; for it's simply unconscious conceit, not to admit frankly that one is a plagiarist.

GOETHE

I

The History
of Ideas

HUMAN UNDERSTANDING is new. Until recent times in the history of this planet, say a hundred thousand years ago or less, there was no talking, no writing, and no thinking, in a human sense. Elaborate methods of communication, perhaps a human version of the dance language of the bees, must already have existed, but there was no articulated speech, no recording of experience in art or script, no stabilization of thought in unit ideas. Man was not yet aware of anything but transitory sensations, presumably not even of himself. His unconscious brain-mind did all the work. Everything man did was without understanding. Yet a process had begun that was to lead to Plato, Newton, Beethoven, and Freud—guided by unconscious factors of whose existence man was ignorant until recently, and which he still does not understand.

3

We may call this the *incomparable adventure*. For dramatic, emotional, and intellectual interest it is unique, once it has seized the mind. Nothing that man can ever conceive can transcend it, for everything that man does and thinks arises from this challenging phenomenon: the unconscious genesis of mental processes, the appearance of thoughts where there were none similar a moment, and none at all a million years, before.

We all partake in this adventure, unconsciously, every minute of our lives. For in everything that we do, in the kitchen, the office, the factory, the study, or anywhere else, the same basic factors, "physical" or "mental," are at work that guided the developing minds of our earliest ancestors. What molds your thoughts and mine at this very moment likewise molded the earliest thoughts of *Homo sapiens*. For there is no reason to assume any basic genetic difference in constitution or general mode of operation (affecting the capacity for a social tradition) between your thinking organ or mine or even Newton's, and that of our ancestors as they developed the art of articulated speech. As Montaigne believed, and biology confirms: *"Chaque homme porte en lui la forme entière de l'humaine condition."* One species, one set of basic structures and potentialities. The incomparable adventure is the story, continuing in each of us now, of the realization step by step of some of those potentialities, through the interaction of imaginative individuals molding new thoughts and a conservative tradition preserving what appears valuable.

If we try for a brief moment to hold in our restricted minds, in our "narrow consciousness," the amplitude of this tremendous adventure of a once unthinking species, aware only of intense transitory sensations, becoming what we are today and knowing what we do, we may be inclined to consider it miraculous or incredible. How can the experience of truth, or beauty, or goodness, arise in a universe that had

not contained it before? How can rational understanding
come into existence and learn to develop itself into logic,
philosophy, and science? How can an unconscious soil produce
the delights and agonies of human life as we know it?

Yet these things may not remain incredible, if we approach
them rightly. The strangeness of this story is partly the result
of emotional prejudice and intellectual error, and of the language we use. Thus we still tend to assume that great achievements are possible only by conscious selection of an aim and
conscious attention to the means of accomplishing it. Certainly that assumption makes the human achievement incredible. But in mid-twentieth century that mistake is
unnecessary; many knew better all the time, as we shall see.
Crystals, plants, and animals grow without any conscious
fuss, and the strangeness of our own history disappears once
we assume that the same kind of natural ordering process that
guides their growth also guided the development of man and
of his mind, and does so still. Man can order, and even communicate, *before* he understands. The history of ideas is
only in small degree a matter of the conscious choice of aims
and methods. If it had to be that, it could not have begun at
all. Ideas are not conscious inferences from experience, but
orderings of experience, achieved largely unconsciously. Consciousness is of great importance, but we do not yet know
where or why.

However, we are not here concerned with the precise status
of "conscious" and "unconscious" factors in the story—which
is not understood—but with a single process: the development
of the human brain-mind as an organ for ordering the records
of the past into symbols and using them to anticipate the
future in a manner serving the development either of the
individual or of the species. And in certain respects the most
powerful symbols are *ideas* representing particular separable
aspects of experience, often expressible as spoken and written

words. Thus the history of ideas, properly understood, is not merely intellectual history, but is an aspect of the complete story of man: biological, developmental, emotional, and social. Ideas and events are inseparable. Indeed the great interest of ideas springs from the fact that they are restricted units of limitless scope: at once clearly separable elements representable in words which can be articulated in chains to provide assertions, and at the same time aspects of experience which spread out into the open realms of emotion and action. This is no paradox, for ideas are nothing more or less than representations of the separable aspects of what is itself unbounded and multiply interrelated. An idea is a focus of unrestricted relationships, just as a point defines an infinity of lines radiating in all directions.

Unfortunately there is as yet no adequate philosophy or science of human history, or even of the development of the human mind. Therefore all that can be done in describing any aspect of the history of ideas is to state the facts as known, and to interpret them as best one can, making one's assumptions explicit as far as possible. Moreover, for the sake of definiteness in a difficult field, we shall here consider only ideas made verbally explicit in literature, though the story might equally be traced in the visual arts.

But ideas about the history of ideas—what sort of inbreeding is that? The history of ideas, in the wider sense used here, should be one of the most fundamental and influential branches of scholarship and teaching, yet to what dangers it is subject! On the one hand, overintellectualism, the undue separation of verbal records and rational ideas from the total history of man. On the other hand, subjectivism, the neglect of detail and the painting of grand dramas in the colors of one mind. Even if the balance is found between these, the subtler difficulty remains that the historian of ideas must watch the false as well as the true consciousness of each period, the dishonest ideologies and rationalizations as well as the unmistakable thread of truth: the molding into words of the organic insights without which there would be no movement toward understanding.

No realm of scholarship demands a greater sense of responsibility and sensitivity to truth, relatively to the lack of agreed criteria to guide the judgment. To be a good historian of ideas it would seem necessary for a writer to be a good man as well as a good thinker; he should not only be clear, precise, and logical, but generous, open, and free: himself an adequate channel for the factors that have brought about the development of the human mind, for they must repeat that process in him.

Yet if the pitfalls are myriad in the history of ideas, so are the signposts when we learn to read them. For given a genuine desire for truth, for the valid order pervading complexity which, being valid, permits advance, the study of the history of ideas generates its own insights and teaches the necessary precautions. This may be seen in the principle, most easily learned from the history of ideas, and stressed by Dilthey, that *all philosophical and scientific doctrines have to be regarded as partial visions of the truth, which we must expect to be replaced one day by more comprehensive ones.* Most conceptions emphasize one aspect only of the truth; conflicting theories are often complementary; the successful doctrine may therefore eventually have to go back to its defeated rivals and learn from them.

This central principle of the history of ideas—that all ideas are partial—is perhaps the most important single fact that the human intellect has yet discovered. It requires interpretation with a modicum of elasticity, for it does not deny that some ideas may fully cover a limited realm—though even here the main principle holds good, since no idea can be used to define its own limitations. Thus the principle remains as the foundation of wisdom: the mind must be modest. Even if it does not, and probably cannot, know its own limitations, it can be aware that they exist. No thinker need accept the onus of perfection.

Does this principle seem obvious? Alas, it is not. One of the dangers of our age, more damaging than ever before, is *total obsession with partial ideas.* The world of pure intellect should be more sensible, but is not. No scholar should present his own ideas, or those of anyone else, as final. This matters today more than ever before, because community and family habits, which used to hold human life relatively stable through the centuries, can no longer be relied on to do so. The present moral vacuum will not long remain empty; no traditional religion can claim universality; classical communism is in decline; some new quasi-religious rationalization of the space age will take over tomorrow, unless those who believe themselves wiser start now by mocking at any total surrender to partial ideas, whether they be those of Marx, or Freud, or anyone else. Let the study of human history help to keep the way clear for the continuing advance of the intellect, by making it unmistakably obvious that every intellectual instrument must sooner or later prove inadequate.

The European and Western ideal of the self-aware individual confronting destiny with his own indomitable will and skeptical reason as the only factors on which he can rely is perhaps the noblest aim which has yet been accepted by any community. This conception of the self-conscious person gave ancient ideals a new characteristically European *élan* and, through its myriad expressions, has been the greatest single influence molding thought and behavior during the last three hundred years. Exact science is one of its many expressions.

But it has become evident that this ideal was a moral mistake and an intellectual error, for it exaggerated the ethical, philosophical, and scientific importance of the awareness of the individual. And one of the main factors exposing this inadequate ideal was the discovery of the unconscious mind. That is why the idea of the unconscious is the supreme revolutionary conception of the modern age: it undermines the traditional foundations of Europe and the West, as was recognized by Windelband [2] as early as 1914 when he expressed concern lest "the hypothesis of the unconscious might destroy certain basic features of our conception of the world." For, in a historical sense, the idea is anti-Classical, anti-European and anti-Enlightenment.

At least this is my interpretation. Indeed I regard the development of contrasted conceptions of unconscious mental processes as an important phase in the emotional and intellectual history of the species. Here the West, through its thinkers, is still leading mankind. Moreover I consider that the time is ripe for an attempt to trace the main features of this phase and to interpret it as a neobiological development, a step toward the fuller exploitation of the innate hereditary faculties of the species. During the last ten years several surveys have been published of the historical background of Freud's ideas, from the Orient and ancient Greece through the medieval mystics to European systematic thinkers. But a review based on assumptions broad enough to permit an interpretation of the whole story has not yet been attempted.

However inadequate the present study, the attempt is necessary. For if my general interpretation is valid, no other single factor is today so fraught with good or evil, with potential benefit or disaster, for mankind. If the human unconscious is one thing, the race is doomed anyway, even without the bombs; if it is another, mankind may conceivably survive present threats and create for itself an unexpected renaissance, not "moral" but biological and human. Furthermore without a balanced conception of the unconscious it is hard to see how human dignity can be restored. For today *faith, if it bears any relation to the natural world, implies faith in the unconscious.* If there is a God, he must speak there; if there is a healing power, it must operate there; if there is a principle of ordering in the organic realm, its most powerful manifestation must be found there. The unconscious mind is the expression of the organic in the individual. But Freud's conception of it is not adequately organic, and the conscious mind will enjoy no peace until it can rejoice in a fuller understanding of its own unconscious sources.

Freud's greatness lies not in any of his particular ideas but in the fact that he compelled the race to face the problem of finding an adequate concept of the unconscious mind. He showed, once and for all, that the unconscious is so powerful that this task cannot be neglected.

If this view is correct another half century should see some headway made. This essay is a contribution from the side of therapeutic history, a suggestion that *all* conceptions of the unconscious have so far been partial, and that the main need is to develop more comprehensive principles covering both the healthy and the pathological, the usual and the unusual, aspects. But, as we shall see later, the antithesis conscious/unconscious may not hold the clue to further advance.

This book is not a study in the history of psychology, tracing how a particular *psychological* idea was developed as the result of experience or observation and of the influence of one writer upon another, with evidence and references supporting each link in a chain of formulations. No definitive study of the history of the idea of the unconscious from this point of view is yet available.

Nor is it concerned with the detailed technical analysis and comparison of the various *philosophical* attitudes which have influenced the development of the idea. This is also a professional task of high complexity, and essays of this kind are already available. It is scarcely surprising that none of these appears satisfactory, since a comprehensive analytical treatment requires an unprejudiced mastery of all relevant philosophical schools.

However, both these tasks lie within established realms of scholarship, and it would be surprising if further endeavors were not made in both directions, or possibly combining the two in a single survey of the development of *philosophical and psychological theories* during the last three hundred years, in relation to the concept of the unconscious mind, say, from Cudworth to Jung.

But such legitimate specialist studies, in order to achieve the maximum of scientific objectivity and intellectual and historical precision, must exclude those matters which are the main concern of this work: the treatment of this feature of the development of the European mind, evidenced in the written word, as a significant phase in the history of man: self-conscious European man discovering his unconscious. Here I do not seek to weigh the relative importance of different contributions, to trace direct or indirect influences, or even to analyze in any detail the distinctions between one concept and another, though a preliminary statement of my preferred ideas will be given in Chapter II. The aim is to outline a changing state of awareness as evidenced in European writings, and to provide detailed, but necessarily incomplete, evidence in support of the general picture, in the form of quotations. I am concerned with the developing awareness, as shown in writings of any kind, of *the need to infer* from the facts of immediate conscious experience *the existence of unconscious mental processes,* and this study is restricted to the particular culture—Europe c. 1680 to 1880—that first gave this inference clear conceptual formulation within a largely dualistic tradition.

Since we cannot reverse the process of history and watch

parents, magic men, priests, or physicians at their daily tasks a thousand or ten thousand years ago so as to judge from their words and actions how far they, consciously or unconsciously, made a similar inference in their treatment of their children, followers, or patients, it is reasonable to start by accepting only the written word as evidence. Moreover, to be adequately sure of the explicit or implicit meaning of words, it is best to rely mainly on words used in senses that one can be sure of understanding. One may think one knows what a mystic or poet writing before A.D. 1000 meant by his words, but can one be certain of appreciating the social and emotional context within which they found their meaning? Even if one believes this possible, an elaborate apparatus of scholarship is necessary to convince others. We shall therefore rely on the written word after A.D. 1600.

In attempting a broad approach to the subject it is useful thus to restrict the historical scope. This does not imply an undervaluation of other cultures and other modes of expression, such as those of ancient Greece, China, or India. My limitation of the field means only that in taking a European story as universally significant the assumption is made that, in its struggle with the systematization of ideas, the European mind during some two hundred years experienced with peculiar intensity and recorded with unique clarity a change of awareness and of emphasis which other cultures probably shared in lesser degree. During two centuries Europe started on a task with which no other culture has ever come seriously to grips.

In passing from scholarly detailed analysis to broad interpretation certain advantages are lost, for precision, objectivity, and reliability become more difficult. But something is also gained.

All human comprehension, whether it be intuitive understanding or scientific explanation, or any blend of these, rests on knowledge with two complementary aspects:

accuracy of detailed facts (precision);

correct arrangement of these into comprehensive generalizations (order).

Neither aspect has any meaning, or relevance to experience, without some element of the other. Facts only become definite in a frame of reference, and an assertion of the existence of some kind of abstract order must be expressed in terms of particular facts to make it meaningful.

Unfortunately, the instability of the human temperament enters here and fogs the issue. European thinkers have tended to split into two camps representing contrasted tendencies in human nature: the one seeking order, similarities, and unity (often called "mystical" or "religious") and the other differences between particulars (the "tough" thinkers or scientists). The first seek comfort in *feeling* a unifying order, the second in the *defining* of particulars. Sometimes members of these opposed camps can scarcely speak to one another, because each stands for what the other has inhibited but uses unconsciously. Yet they represent complementary differentiations of one underlying tendency present in all human thought: *the search for order in particular facts*. Here the term "order" stands for some form of unity, similarity, regularity, or equivalence, and any such order is subject to definite restrictions. For no form of order is universal, and a statement of any "truth" is only acceptable when it explicitly defines the conditions under which it is true, to the satisfaction of contemporary critics.

No scientific assertion is legitimate unless it makes clear the general ordering principles on which it is based, and this is often neglected. On the other hand, a broad interpretation of some nonscientific realm usually cannot avoid making its prior assumptions clear to the reader. Thus a personal interpretation may be less treacherous than a supposedly scientific one which conceals the problematic character of its hidden assumptions.

But can a personal interpretation of historical facts ever

possess any degree of validity? I believe it can, because the
sense of truth, the critical judgment, can be improved by
training. Moreover, if by "truth" we mean an ordering of
particular facts which permits further advance, then the sense
of truth prevails more often than not. Given undeformed
organic vigor, the senses and the ordering mind operate
reasonably well, on the average and in the long run. The
organ of thought tends to improve its own operations, on a
long personal or historical view. If this had not been the case,
there could have been no community life, no language, no
rational thought, no science. Moreover it is precisely this
élan toward clarity and validity that leads us to criticize its
manifold failures and pathologies. The conception of error
proves a standard implicit in the working of the mind, and
the achievements of the Western intellect and of exact science
show that a collective tradition and discipline can strengthen
the mind's faculty of self-criticism. This implies that a personal interpretation of a particular aspect of history, such
as that set out in Chart A,* though it may be in some degree a
projection of personal experience, can also be more than that,
for if each man carries in him the entire human condition
one man's story may reflect history. (When aware of introducing a personal assumption I write "I"; when opening a
dialogue with the reader I use "we.")

The story told here presupposes certain principles regarding the history of ideas:

There is no one *Zeitgeist,* no single state of awareness in
any community, even in a small professional group, at any
one time. There may be traditional elements in decline, a
variety of dominant elements, and new ones emerging. Moreover the awareness of any single individual varies according
to what he has in hand at the moment.

* This refers to the first of three charts (A, B, and C) to be found at the back
of the book.

In the life history of ideas a similar variety is present. There is often one period when a new idea is *conceivable*, as evidenced by the printed word; another when it becomes *topical*, as shown by multiple discussions; and sometimes another when it becomes manifestly *effective*. Moreover ideas may undergo cycles of influence, and may be temporarily inhibited, and consciously, or unconsciously, transformed.

One phase in the life history of an idea is of special relevance to our topic. This may be called its *climax*, when it is widely acclaimed and is accepted by nearly everyone, but its value is already declining, though this is only known to a few. The prestige of an idea may be as misleading as the reputation of a man. When young men or ideas are most fertile they are usually unrecognized by their community. Once prestige or reputation is established the main task is often over; only the greatest ideas or men can continue to be fertile in the new context which they have themselves helped to create.

If an idea is of universal relevance many kinds of thinkers, and different groups, will respond to the need for it in their own ways. The school of thought which is apparently most directly opposed to it may be the first to give it explicit consideration, just because the need for what their thinking entirely lacks is strongly felt, at least by some of its members. *Les extrèmes se touchent.*

Ideas are not discovered once and for all and passed on like museum objects. They are part of the life of thought and must come to life, be kept alive, and be made productive in the processes of human minds and the activities of individuals. The same ideas, or similar ones, may have to be independently rediscovered over and over again by isolated thinkers, some of whom may never communicate their thoughts, while others may have spoken but not been understood or produced any recorded response, and finally by still others who bring the idea to full life, not only in their own minds but in a professional or social community. The world as a whole, ignorant of this long story in some particular case, may stand amazed at the "power of genius." For his words or creations throb with the excitement of his own discovery, and his heat sets them on fire. His discovery appears magical to him, and so to his audience. He could not possibly have withstood the burden of his task had he known that countless others had already thought in similar ways. He must make the discovery for himself and not find it in a book, if the idea is to live in him and in his work, and through him in others.

The interpretation offered here of one aspect of the recent history of the Western mind does not involve "historical determinism" in any sense implying either that prediction is trivial or that the experience of free will is illusory. Nonetheless, the anticipation of future possibilities on the basis of largely unconscious assumptions is one of the main biological functions of the ordering processes in the human brain, and veridical historical prophecy is frequently possible.

This book offers an interpretation based on facts. The interpretation is given in Chapters I–IV. In the present chapter I have outlined some principles which I consider should guide the study of the history of ideas. Chapter II describes my preferred interpretation of the terms "conscious" and "unconscious," and of the factors producing awareness. Chapter III describes how, in my view, such factors made individuals in Europe intensely aware of themselves before and after 1600, and Chapter IV how they later became aware of the need to infer the existence of unconscious mental processes. The next four chapters cite some of the thinkers who made this inference. Chapter IX summarizes the present position and poses some questions.

II

Conscious and Unconscious

As A. B. JOHNSON [3] wrote in 1836: "Nature is no party to our phraseology." Certainly the terms "conscious," "unconscious," "subconscious," and "preconscious," though valuable, are not entirely satisfactory. The trouble is not that they are ambiguous; that might be overcome by providing better definitions. It is that we do not yet know the right definitions to use, the meanings which would throw most light on the structure of mental processes. What we need is not merely words with definitions using other words, but insight into the changing structure of mental processes. Until we can identify a law covering all mental processes, definitions cannot do more than flatter us into imagining we are thinking properly, when we are not.

It may, for example, be wrong to think of two *realms* which interact, called the conscious and the unconscious, or even of two contrasted kinds of mental *process*, conscious and unconscious, each causally self-contained until it hands over to the other. There may exist, as I believe, a single realm of mental processes, continuous and mainly unconscious, of which only certain transitory aspects or phases are accessible to immediate conscious attention. On this view there are few, if any, causally separable "conscious processes"; only particular features or transitory phases of mental processes enter direct awareness.

The main purpose of this study is to outline the development of human self-awareness; to emphasize its special quality and intensity around 1600 in Europe; and to trace in more detail the progressive recognition, in the systematic thought which developed after Galileo, Kepler, and Descartes, that it is necessary to infer that mental factors which are not directly available to our awareness influence both our behavior and the conscious aspects of our thought.

In telling such a story, unless one is satisfied with a bare listing of historical facts, some assumptions are unavoidable regarding the genesis and nature of conscious and unconscious factors, and the best meanings of these terms. Why did men gradually become aware of themselves as experiencing individuals? Why did they later feel the need to infer the existence of unconscious mental factors? We do not know the answers, but each can use the facts to form his own opinion. Since this survey is an expression of my view I feel bound to make it explicit.

That alone might not justify some pages of speculative theory. But I cannot criticize the Cartesian dualism without suggesting a path that may lead toward a better way of thinking, throwing light on the "interactions" which dualistic thinking leaves obscure. So I ask the reader either to be patient with the next few pages or to pass at once to the later part of this chapter. Those who do not share the logical thinker's anxiety for precision may find these pages tedious, though they underlie much that follows.

I have thus far used the terms "conscious" and "unconscious" in a vague sense. I shall now indicate what I consider to be the best usages, the meanings that may form part of a future mental science, insofar as this antithesis remains useful. For the succeeding chapters interpret the history of the discovery of the unconscious in the way in which I believe it should be done by a future science of mind.

We shall move step by step from general principles to special features of unconscious mental processes and their conscious aspects. The analysis here is logical and theoretical; the historical treatment of the development of European man from overemphasis of self-consciousness to recognition of the unconscious is the subject of the later chapters. Each of the following numbered paragraphs treats a theme which is summarized in italics. The formulations are tentative; their brevity and apparent precision do not imply dogmatism. But they appear to be useful working assumptions.

1. We require a single method of approach which avoids the partly verbal problem of the relations of "matter" and "mind," and deals with the changing structure of experienced and observed relationships. *It will therefore be assumed that a unified theory is possible, and lies ahead, in which "material" and "mental," "conscious" and "unconscious," aspects will be derivable as related components of one primary system of ideas.* We need not consider here in what respects this single system of thought may be "neutral" as between the physical and the subjective languages.

2. It will further be assumed that this future theory of mental processes will constitute a special application of a more general theory of organism, and this in turn of a still more general theory of the transformations of partly ordered com-

plex systems, based on a universal postulate that *in isolable systems disorder tends to decrease.* ("Disorder" may be defined as the number of theoretically independent parameters necessary to describe the system at any moment, and this "ordering principle" defines the class of systems which can be treated as isolable for purposes of causal description under this principle.)

This postulate alone gives significance to our definitions. Any process illustrating it will be called *ordering* or *formative.* Here the Platonic "forms" are generalized to become actual tendencies in the world of process, as recognized by Aristotle but still to be clarified by science.

3. On this view *most organisms may be described as hierarchical systems of ordering processes,* their self-replicating activity being the extension of their characteristic type of ordering by the transformation of structures absorbed from their environment. Similarly, "mental" processes are the expression of an ordering tendency evident *both* in a complete physiological description of the processes of the central nervous system and the brain, *and* in a subjective description of directly experienced states. These preliminaries enable us to pass to the definitions we require.

4. *"Mental process" will be used to mean the dominant ordering process (in an animal with a brain) in which the traces of past or present individual experience are themselves ordered, and tend to order current or anticipated behavior under the dominant vital drives.* The traces of experience are often records of distinctions or contrasts. Such mental ordering processes tend to involve some degree of modification both of the established mental orderings and of the new traces. The mental ordering process is a plastic activity which may deform or simplify the records in the course of organizing them.

Conscious will be used to mean *directly present in aware-*

ness (or "immediately known to awareness"). This adjective will be applied only to discrete *aspects* or brief *phases* of mental processes. No distinction will be made between "conscious" and "aware." Except for a few doubtful extreme cases (e.g., processes of logical or mathematical deduction) there appear to be no causally self-contained processes of which all aspects directly enter awareness. "Conscious" is a subjective term without, as yet, (i) interpretation in terms of physiological structure, or (ii) explanation of its function.

Unconscious,[4] in the term "unconscious mental processes" will be used to mean *all mental processes except those discrete aspects or brief phases which enter awareness as they occur.* Thus "unconscious mental processes" (or the "unconscious," for short) is here used as a comprehensive term including not only the "subconscious" and "preconscious," but all mental factors and processes of which we are not immediately aware, whatever they be: organic or personal tendencies or needs, memories, processes of mimicry, emotions, motives, intentions, policies, beliefs, assumptions, thoughts, or dishonesties.

Where precision is desirable "conscious" and "unconscious" will not be used as nouns. The continuous unconscious sections and the discrete conscious aspects of mental processes are intimately interconnected, as components of the total realm of mental processes. A single integrated transformation proceeds in a single organ: the mind-brain. This mental process follows its own laws and is frequently an ordering process; discrete features of this process may "become conscious" or "be the subject of conscious attention."

"Awareness," when present, may be awareness of an external sense perception or of an internal sensation or other experience. It is not necessary here to consider various special or pathological types of awareness, as in dreams, hallucinations, etc.

5. *The structure of mental processes.* Mental processes are complex; hierarchically organized; finalistic, i.e., tending toward some terminus (though certain mental operations are reversible); involve memory, selection, and the formative or ordering imagination; and usually serve biological, social, or individual ends. Since the operation of memory, selection, and the ordering imagination characterize all mental processes, *poetic fantasy* may be taken as a representative example, while *logical deduction* (including mathematical calculation) is a special case, lacking the selective and formative aspects.

If we neglect their hierarchical organization, which is not yet understood, *the characteristic structure of mental processes is that of an ordering process, in which traces are so organized as to guide present or future thought and behavior.*

As the result of special conditions (excessive strain, etc.) the hierarchical organized unity of the system of mental processes may be disrupted, dissociated, or otherwise disorganized. But if favorable conditions are restored, the ordering tendency may have the power to re-establish the unified state.

6. *Factors promoting awareness.* The following suggestions summarize the results of recent research. But all conclusions are tentative until more is known of the distinction between the differentiated or focused awareness, e.g., of one external sense perception like the sight of a point, and the awareness of a complex situation involving an extensive field and several senses, like the awareness of all the sights, sounds, and smells perceived from a window.

It seems that differentiated awareness often accompanies the operation of distance perceptors (vision, hearing, smell) and of the highest integrating processes of the neural hierarchy absorbing information from these senses, so as to anticipate the effect of possible responses. But this condition is not necessary. One can be aware of pleasant memories which neither involve the external senses nor evoke any response. It seems that any trace, new or old, which enters the dominant nervous processes can evoke awareness. However the meaning of "dominance" is obscure.

It is evident that sharpness, novelty, surprise, challenge, pain (below a threshold), and pleasure may all promote awareness. But none of these factors is a necessary condition of awareness. Since most, if not all, awareness involves discrimination, or consciousness of a contrast or distinction, we shall provisionally assume that *conscious aspects of mental processes are distinctions affecting the momentarily dominant ordering processes; the content of awareness is the tension of a contrast.* This defines a program of research: to discover the meaning of "dominant" in terms of structure and function. We are definitely conscious at any one moment only of a few relatively stable contrasts, and unconscious of the vast changing complexity of which they form part. The senses discriminate; the (unconscious) mind orders.

One basic problem is, how can contrasts be ordered? The logician has to consider how dissimilars can be correlated, the biologist how differentiated structures and processes are co-ordinated within the organism, and the brain physiologist and psychologist how the mind discovers an order in the contrasts which it observes.

7. *The role of awareness.* Awareness wanders, is transitory and often interrupted, and ranges from a differentiated consciousness of isolated factors to a vague sense of the rhythm of being alive. The biological function of awareness is still uncertain, but appears to be narrower than has often been thought.

The function of awareness is linked with that of the dominant integrating processes of the nervous system and its site (if any), or sites, may wander from one part of the brain to another. "Dominance," it seems, is often associated with a wandering distinction, without permanent location, temporal continuity, or even one unchanging character, since it can be either sharp or diffused.

But it is clear that *conscious attention* often heightens the clarity of discrimination and quickens the achievement of an adequate delayed response. The stronger the awareness of some factor, the more definite its separation as something requiring its own response. Only awareness can, in principle, call directly on all the reserves of experience; it is a signal echoing through all the available associations of memory. Yet it need not await an external stimulus, for awareness can play on internal factors.

Since we do not yet understand biological organization in general, or its particular case, neural integration, it is not surprising that we cannot define either the precise role of awareness or the objective physiological situation to which it corresponds (though electrical studies of the brain have come close to this problem). But it is clear that *intensity of awareness is heightened by the degree of novelty, and of challenge to the person, of some perceived contrast.* It may be lessened again when an adequate response, often an ordering of the new contrast into a modified personal or social order, has been achieved. Thus awareness of this contrast self/environment is normally *self-eliminating,* in the sense that in producing an adequate response it eliminates the factor which evoked it. The role of the characteristically human *self*-consciousness may be to facilitate those responses which require considerable time because they involve a substantial adjustment of the established order.

The significance of these provisional conclusions for the theme of this book is that one may expect individuals to have their conscious attention drawn particularly to any novel contrasts which challenge the established ordering of their lives or of their thought. We shall use this principle to describe and interpret the historical development of two particular forms of awareness:

Self-awareness of the person, in which the attention of the individual is drawn to his own faculty of experiencing. This process is too vast to be treated other than in outline here. We are concerned only with one expression of it: European man's use of words to describe his own self-reflective awareness.

The discovery of the unconscious, in the sense of the self-aware European becoming aware of the need to *infer* from his direct experiences the existence of mental processes in himself of which he is not immediately aware, and to employ a special term for these unconscious processes.

I have here outlined some of the ideas which, adequately clarified, should, in my view, underlie a unified theory of mental processes. But psychology has not yet established any such unified doctrine and this historical study is concerned only with one step already taken toward that aim: the partial correction, through the "discovery of the unconscious," of the error of treating the individual self-consciousness as primary.

This is part of a larger story: the slow development of self-awareness in the human species, and its accompaniment by a dim sense, gradually growing more definite, of divine or natural agencies guiding and controlling the actions and thoughts of the individual. In that story biology and anthropology must set the background, and the parts played by the earliest civilizations, in particular those of ancient Egypt, Greece, China, and India, be given their place. It may be that Europe has not developed any ideas of which the germ is not to be found elsewhere in earlier times. More than that, both this "European" error and its correction may be latent in the history of Greek, Indian, or Chinese thought. It would be surprising if that were not the case.

Our theme is universal, but here we are only concerned with its expression in European minds with the bias, displayed mainly after 1600, toward the systematic and later the scientific, exploitation of words. In fact our story begins after Descartes (1596–1650) and the publication of his *Discourse* (1637). That work marks a crucial moment in the history of ideas, for it initiated the writings in which Descartes sought to stabilize with final clarity an ancient dualism: the split of subject from object. Archeological remains dating some 10,000 years back suggest that men had then begun to discriminate an ideal eternal soul from the frail and perishable body. Moreover many religious and early philosophers, Plato for example, assumed a similar separation of soul or mind from the material universe. But Descartes was the first thinker to assert a sharp division of mind from matter as the basis of a systematic philosophy claiming scientific clarity and certainty.

To postulate the existence of two separate realms of being, one of which is characterized by awareness, as Descartes did, may prove one of the fundamental blunders made by the human mind. However admirable his genius, and however fertile the dualistic approach has been, Descartes' claim to clarity renders him the exemplar of this treacherous dualism. Our theme is the development of the conception of "unconscious mental processes" as a first correction of that Cartesian blunder, the denial of the existence of an independent realm discriminated by awareness. All the writers whom I shall quote (after 1650) say, in effect, either: "If there are two realms, physical and mental, awareness cannot be taken as the criterion of mentality," or, going further: "The assumption of two separate realms is untenable, for the unity displayed in their interactions is more important than their separation."

Descartes recognized that the "union of soul with body" is intuitively known, and that their pervasive connections are a matter of everyday experience. However, in his doctrine these connections are not ones of true causation, but an illusion resulting from some kind of parallelism between the two modes of being. It is therefore, in Descartes' view, abortive to study these connections in detail.

He has widely been regarded, and with justice, as the supreme representative of the dualistic view. Yet his own thinking did not in fact possess the clarity that he claimed. His ideas seemed clear to him only because he inhibited, or postponed for later consideration, inconvenient facts.

One part of his mind, impatient for logical clarity, thought: "the soul is of a nature wholly independent of the body" (*Discourse*), and "it is certain that I am really distinct from my body and can exist without it" (*Meditations*). But he was also a careful observer, and another part of his mind thought: "The mind is so intimately dependent on the condition and relations of the organs of the body that if any means can ever be found to render men wiser and more ingenious than hitherto, I believe it is in Medicine they must be sought for" (*Discourse*).

Descartes the Cartesian was a product of intellectual impatience; Descartes the observer recognized that the pervasive interactions remained a challenge to understanding and offered an opportunity for therapy. But he left it to others to explain why clear fundamental ideas leave so much obscure.

Prior to Descartes and his sharp definition of the dualism there was no cause to contemplate the possible existence of unconscious mentality as part of a separate realm of mind. Many religious and speculative thinkers had taken for granted factors lying outside but influencing immediate awareness; Augustine's remarks on memory are a famous example. Until an attempt had been made (with apparent success) to choose *awareness* as the defining characteristic of an independent mode of being called mind, there was no occasion to invent the idea of *unconscious* mind as a provisional correction of that choice. It is only after Descartes that we find, first the idea and then the term, "unconscious mind" entering European thought.

There was nothing remarkable in the ancient view that both divine and physical agencies could influence the mind; that only seemed philosophically disturbing after Descartes had converted many to his view that conscious mentality should be separated from everything else. It may be that part of the appeal of Freud's ideas was due to the fact that he did more than anyone before him toward repairing the dualism into which the thought of most educated Europeans had fallen since the seventeenth century. For Freud's influence has been greatest in the Protestant English-speaking world, and it was here that the dualism penetrated furthest.

Thus the most profound aspect of Freud's hold over many minds may have little to do with his scientific discoveries, with sex, or libido, or any special aspect of the unconscious, except as an opportunity for the conscious subject to escape his isolation, for the individual to relax his lonely self-awareness in a surrender to what is organic and universal. This deep appeal can be expressed in philosophical terms: by calling attention to the unconscious mental processes Freud gave the Western world an opportunity to improve the relations of the individual as subject to nature as object, in the daily life of ordinary people as well as in the thinking of the clinics and the academies. I know no better way in which to understand the fascination which Freud's name, ideas, and writings hold for so many in the English-speaking world. He has helped us to recognize the need and the possibility of escaping from a disastrous intellectual and moral split that has caused trouble for all individuals and cultures that have flirted with this facile disordering of experience.

Quintillian wrote: *"Scientia difficultatem facit"* (the theory creates the difficulties). No difficulties have been so profound or so persistent as those which reason has made for itself by its hasty separation of the conscious self from everything else. The impatience to order has here led to disorder.

III

The Rise of European Self-Awareness

OUR STORY TAKES PLACE in Europe after A.D. 1600 and expresses in condensed form universal human potentialities. Certain persisting hereditary characteristics of the species made possible the development of mind, the genesis of self-awareness, and the recent discovery that the primary mental processes are unconscious. We do not yet understand these basic organic characteristics. But in the previous chapter I have offered a way of viewing mental processes and their origin, because without this the story would lose its continuity and fall apart into an arbitrary sequence of miracles.

Though we can have no direct knowledge of the growth of consciousness in past times it is reasonable to assume that such moments of awareness that gregarious animals enjoy, or that the earliest members of *Homo sapiens* experienced, are relatively transitory and undifferentiated aspects of continuous social activities, associated in general with a lesser range of conscious memory and anticipation than that of which we are capable today. Through a process occupying many thousands of generations, the later stages of which were probably linked with the development of articulated speech, men gradually became more often and more definitely *self*-conscious, dimly aware of a persisting experiencing self, with its own continuity of memory, distinguishable from objects perceived around them. What is here inadequately described in elaborate terms was a spontaneous intuitive discrimination, unconsciously inferred from the structure of awareness, an attempt made without deliberation to find an order in immediate experience, stimulated at those moments when experience seemed to display this dual structure. At least that seems a reasonable inference from known facts.

This splitting of experience into two aspects: my awareness and the world, which eventually led to dualistic ways of thinking, presumably emerged very slowly and tended to occur chiefly at moments of danger or surprise when some prior unified and less conscious ordering of experience proved inadequate. The individual probably only performed this mental act of separating himself from everything else when the facts tended to force this on him. The intuitive sense of a persisting experiencing self constitutes a treacherous basis for an ordering of experience, because the direct awareness of the human individual does not justify the attribution to the self either of *permanence,* or of *unchanging identity,* or of *continuous awareness.* Indeed the facts of growth, aging, and death, and the transitory wandering character of awareness render this assumption of a permanent identical conscious subject most peculiar. Why did the human mind ever make such a strange, apparently perverse, "inference"?

The hypostatization of a permanent self cannot have been

due either to the conscious vanity of the individual or to his fear of death, for these are its consequences and cannot be its causes. It is probable that the basic factor, in all the leading Western communities whose languages reveal an exaggerated isolation of the self from change, was the widespread but not universal tendency of the mind to treat its own mental traces as representations of permanent entities. This tendency is not surprising, since most separate stable traces are precisely the rendering permanent, in the form of a record, of some aspect of a persisting or recurrent experience. As Bergson noted: "Our concepts have been formed on the model of solids." We shall return again to this point, for it dominates our story.

It is all the more interesting, therefore, that certain African and American Indian communities, the Hopi and others, appear to put the cognitive emphasis, not on separable traces representing isolable entities, but on the actual process of personal experiencing. Whorf [5] has suggested that their languages are molded to represent the *transformation of the subject* in the course of his experienced activities and of his participation in the processes of his world. The Hopi, for example, view reality as "events," rather than as "matter." These languages, far from being vague or undifferentiated, make finer discriminations in regard to the action of thinking than do the European. They are highly developed systems of communication, stressing a different aspect of experience.

None the less these languages of process and participation do not help to promote the awareness by the individual of his characteristic personality and its capacities and needs. *Stable contrasts* are less clearly focused, a vague *unity of process* tending to dominate mental activities. Thus it seems that the first step toward a precise structural understanding of the variety of phenomena must be through the exploitation of permanent separable contrasted aspects, which is what the individual traces normally represent. On this view the sharp separation of subject from object, first intuitively and later in European rational analysis, was not perverse, but a necessary stage toward a fuller realization of the potentialities of the human intellect.

However that may be, as the vital surplus in man led to the gradual development of his mental faculties, the separation of a conscious self from an objective universe became inevitable in vigorous communities once the resistance of the world around to the needs of the human individual and group forced this contrast and challenge on his attention. The biological "function," in a generalized sense, of this awareness was to assist man in eliminating the clash by modifying either the environment or the activities of the person, and thus to remove the conditions which evoked the moment of self-awareness. The clear awareness of a distinction self/environment tended to facilitate adequate delayed responses which would lessen the clash and hence to relax the self-awareness. Thus *self-awareness is basically self-eliminating;* its biological function is apparently to catalyze processes which tend to remove its cause, in each situation. Consciousness is like a fever which, if not excessive, hastens curative processes and so eliminates its source. Hence its transitory, wandering, and often strangely unreasonable character. Contrasted with the growth of a plant or an animal, persisting self-awareness is like an illness which continually provokes its own cure, and in the long run usually does so. (Only *aesthetic* awareness, in which there is no consciousness of the self contrasted with the environment, is not self-eliminating.)

We may conveniently define an extreme representative type, *self-conscious man,* as the individual who is excessively self-aware, does not understand the etiology or limitations of this condition, and treats self-awareness not as a sequence of self-eliminating moments of fever, but as primary in theory, in value, or in action. "Self-conscious man" is a useful abstraction, and also an idea which, as we shall see, proved attractive to many Europeans from around 1600 onward. One can think of several representative figures of the last three centuries in whom the natural moments of fever became a persisting pathological condition. For example, Goethe suffered from an exceptionally intense and continuous self-awareness, but it was relieved by his wide range of interests and disciplined by equally continuous work.

The condition of self-conscious man is efficient in promoting thought and action, particularly in new explorations of all kinds, and it produced among other things a vigorous transitional development of the rational intellect. But it has also led to two serious embarrassments, for a valid ordering of experience cannot be based on the uncritical acceptance of the responses of an organ, or organic condition, *which directs its main attention to contrasts* and *is self-eliminating*.

1. It leads to a biased estimate of human life. In attending to contrasts, consciousness stresses the disorders, conflicts, clashes, and inadequacies, and tends to neglect the harmonies. Pain and conflict provoke our concentrated attention and difficulties are magnified, while the free play of spontaneous vitality—as in the transitory rhythms of eating, drinking, walking, loving, making things, working well, thinking, and dreaming—evokes no persistent differentiated awareness. We feel right while it is going on, and then forget it, as a rule.

It is a tough fact of the human constitution that it displays a tendency to neglect, or take for granted as unworthy of attention, perfectly ordered processes, and to concentrate on contrasts, differences, lacks, and forms of disorder. This is evident, for example, in the absence of any general concept or word (outside the language of mysticism) for *perfection in process,* in spite of the fact that perfectly coordinated complex processes have been going on for a thousand million years in all living cells, and are occurring by myriads at this very moment in your body and mine. Perfection of ordered transformations is more than a biological commonplace, it is an almost universal fact. In technical terms, the probability of this perfection within living cells is nearly unity, the chance of some transformation going wrong being incredibly minute, say one in countless billions for young organisms in a favorable environment. This alone has made possible the continuity of life over a thousand million years and given living systems the chance of doing more than merely continue to be what they already were. Life can develop, mutate, evolve, and in man create without visible limits, only because it rests on a *perfect foundation,* for practical purposes in terms of the species and race.

It is strange that the West does not yet possess a simple term for "order or harmony in process"; perhaps if it had felt the need to invent one, self-conscious man would have been a little less liable to live and die in a state of frustration and disappointment. But as it is, in treating his own self-awareness as primary and not as a secondary condition whose role is to eliminate what caused the awareness by some adaptive modification either of the environment or of himself, he is often doomed to misery. Many of the most productive personalities have been cursed with a haunting sense of failure, their intense activities being unduly forced by preoccupation with their ego.

For self-conscious man, as here conceived, cannot be whole-natured. This has been known to philosophers, mystics, psychologists, and ordinary men and women of all times: learn to know yourself by all means, when you feel it necessary, but then turn to something in which you can forget yourself. We see ancient wisdom laboriously becoming modern science in a recognition of the human function of awareness: the elimination of its causes. It is not merely civilization which "advances by extending the number of important operations which we can perform without thinking about them," as Whitehead said, but the individual also. The main purpose of conscious thought, its neobiological function, may be first to identify, and then to eliminate, the factors which evoke it.

2. This private embarrassment, the individual's conscious overemphasis on disorder, might matter less if it were not linked to a second which is its social and intellectual counterpart: valid rational understanding of man and nature cannot be reached by treating as primary what is self-eliminating and therefore normally transient. It is philosophically inconceivable that so slippery a feature as consciousness could hold the clue to an ordering of anything. This assumption had to be challenged at once if self-conscious man was not to lead Western thought into further abstract confusion. And precisely that happened. We shall see that within fifty years of the publication of Descartes' first essay, at the very moment when the Cartesian doctrine emphasizing man's consciousness attained its greatest influence, the process of correction was already at work.

Thus a problem arose in the seventeenth century which I shall call the *dilemma of self-conscious man:* being self-aware he required a far-reaching conscious understanding in order to live appropriately to his own nature, but his mind was in a transitional condition for he did not yet recognize the secondary self-eliminating function of his awareness and he attempted to treat its signals as primary for thought and action. However, the direct messages of consciousness are not functionally self-sufficient, and man's self-awareness is not itself an independent controlling organ. It is one differentiated aspect only of the total organ of mind, important for the identification and ordering of contrasts, yet never the ultimate determinant of any ordering process, in thought or behavior. The decisive factors, the primary decisions, are unconscious.

The appearance of this type of individual in increasing numbers or the increasing influence of this ideal at any time is evidence that the human tradition—a varying blend of habit, myth, ritual, religion, philosophy, and science—is no longer adequate in relation to man's developing activities. The momentary self- and object-awareness of an earlier period expressible as "*I* am looking at some strange *object;* what is it?" becomes a sustained social condition: "*I* am experiencing this strange affair of human life; what does it signify, since no doctrine can tell me?" evident in germ in Boehme, Montaigne, Pascal, and Kierkegaard, and today a commonplace.

Why this happened at particular periods is a difficult question, outside our present theme. It is enough to recognize that the new modes of acting and thinking which provoke such searching questions are the expression of a vital surplus which goes beyond adaptation to the immediate demands of current situations. The root source of everything that has contributed to the development of human potentialities is this biological surplus energy, vital discontent, exploratory future-oriented urge, expressed in the anticipatory character of all thought.

The dog that enjoys playing and the monkey that finds pleasure in tackling soluble problems suggest that a biology of behavior relying on narrowly adaptive or utilitarian principles, based merely on rewards or the release of tension, may be too narrow. Organisms promote their own complete rhythms, the increase as well as the decrease of tensions. Man himself displays the absurdity of such narrow theories for he enjoys difficulties, seeks trouble, and is challenged by the apparently impossible. He will go to any length to escape his hated self-awareness. Sometimes he will even surrender himself, or his conscious pride, in the discovery of whole-natured activities. And if thought is his line, and the pathology of self-consciousness has not gone too far, he will even recognize the primacy of his unconscious mind.

It is not known how this condition of human self-awareness was first developed as a reorientation of man's perceptive functions, the proprioceptive senses turning inward toward the organ of thought. Little is to be gained by studying the genesis of self-awareness in the growing child, for that is a secondary process, its parents teaching it to think of itself as they do of themselves. The first sources of the condition lie hidden not in childhood today, but far in the historical past.

We can obtain some light on this by considering contemporary "primitive" peoples whose customs or languages emphasize the role of the individual less than ours. The anthropologist Radin [6] suggested that "every human group . . . has, from time immemorial, contained individuals who were constrained by their individual temperaments and interests to occupy themselves with the basic problems . . . of philosophy." In Radin's view every community, since the birth of human languages, contained a small proportion of original thinkers, men who thought for themselves about their own experience and sensed the inadequacy of traditional ways. Such men must surely at moments have meditated on the difference between themselves and others, and possessed in a greater degree than their fellows the self-reflective consciousness. But the experience of competition for food or for a mate, of painful illness, or of approaching death, must often have stimulated a similar self-awareness.

It would be misleading to select any early historical personality and to suggest that he was the *earliest* individual who is *known* to have experienced an intense sustained self-awareness similar to our own. For the earlier the choice, the less surely is this known.

Nonetheless it is useful to consider an early case, as an

illustration of the conditions which may have provoked an exceptional degree of self-awareness, and I know of none better than Akhenaton (Amenhotep IV, 1388–1358 B.C., Pharaoh of the Egyptian Empire from 1375–1358; dates probably correct within five years). Breasted called him the "world's first individual," and this has a useful meaning. Even when allowance is made for the continuity in Akhenaton's social environment, family origins, and historical setting, the art and scripts of his reign suggest that he was so original, so unlike any predecessor known to have been similarly situated, that he must have experienced an intense and sustained sense of his own uniqueness, of his unusual mission, and probably of his historical "failure." One can hardly avoid conceiving him as a highly self-conscious person, vividly aware that his own nature compelled him to follow strange paths, for he sought to uproot one religion and to establish another, he built a new capital at Amarna to symbolize this change and, though supremely powerful, he refused to make war to save his Empire. He may have been a neurotic epileptic and politically weak; he certainly displayed originality of an order for which there is no precedent in the known records. The inference that he was also for periods intensely self-conscious is no less reliable than many which we draw every day. For he must surely have been vividly aware of the conflict between his own nature and his environment.

Though we cannot trace the origins or development of self-consciousness with any certainty, with the improvement of the records from 5000 B.C. onward we find more and more individuals making their mark on the human story as we know it. This is a fascinating theme, still, I believe, awaiting comprehensive treatment, but it is not ours here. We must step across some thirty centuries following Akhenaton to consider in outline the remarkable transformation of human ways which began in Europe, for reasons which are partly obscure, around A.D. 1100–1200, and reached a crucial stage in the decades before and after A.D. 1600. During this period many habits and traditions began to collapse, the Christian tendency to accept the *status quo* lost its prestige, and self-conscious man (as we have defined him) began to take over the leadership. Ancient ways only survived insofar as they were modified and reinterpreted by imaginative individuals. The person thinking for himself ceased to be a social freak inhibited by his difference from others, and began to claim the opportunity to realize himself and to guide the community. This change is shown in the upper part of Chart A.

The selection of A.D. 1600 requires no justification here. But a few dates may serve to illustrate the outburst of individual vitality which challenged traditional ways around that time. In the background there was the renewed attention to classical scripts from the twelfth century onward and the consequences of the European discovery of printing in the fifteenth century. Hamlet was written in 1598/9, Kepler met Tycho de Brahe in 1600, Descartes started thinking afresh in 1619, and the "Mayflower" set out in 1620. The individual was becoming more interested in the facts of human nature, particularly those accessible to his or her own introspection: Santa Teresa of Avila (1515–1582), Montaigne (1533–1592), Kepler (1571–1630), Boehme (1575–1624), Pascal (1632–1662), Rousseau (1712–1778). Religious thinkers felt the need to develop their personal experience of God, philosophers to express their own vision of the facts. This break with orthodoxy was by 1700 becoming widely accepted in the incipient movements of individualism, liberalism, democracy, rationalism, and scientific skepticism. As Brennan has said, "pride was the vice of the seventeenth century," and beneath all these special manifestations lay the intensified self-awareness of the individual.

In that century we can recognize the germ of a new experience and a new way of living which in our own time has become a social commonplace: the existentialist complaint that there is no tradition which makes life bearable. Already then the sensitive individual knew himself to be deserted; parent, teacher, and adolescent, first unconsciously and later with a deep guilt or resentment, recognized that there existed no single manifestly adequate tradition. The ugly fact was in the open: the old had failed the young. From then onward every sensitive and vital young person had to make his own choice. Once he became aware of this freedom and necessity, the alternatives before him were many. To mention only a few: he could go to the East and become a Buddhist; decide that skeptical reason and scientific method held all the clues; take any other available path; believe in nothing. Or, like Shakespeare, he could accept the music and the tempest, and hold the mirror to man. This date with destiny had been experienced before, but never with such necessity and freedom as from 1600. The challenge was unavoidable, and the absence of effective precedents and rules intensified the lonely self-awareness of the new kind of man.

The seventeenth century was the first period when the individual's experience of "consciousness" and "self-consciousness" was isolated and treated as a primary concept or value, the first principle of universal philosophies and the essential attribute of divinity, though, in a different context, this attitude had been implicit in Socrates and Plato. With a naïveté which has its charm in restrospect, a few thinkers, such as Fichte somewhat later, went so far as to enthrone awareness, this moody and promiscuous visitor, as the sole basis of reality.

Thought and language mold each other, and the heightened attention to the awareness of the individual is evidenced in the fact that words expressing awareness and self-awareness first emerge in the English and German languages during the seventeenth century. In English "conscious" as meaning "inwardly sensible or aware" appears first in 1620, "consciousness" or "the state of being conscious" in 1678, and "self-consciousness" or "consciousness of one's own thoughts, etc." in 1690. In German the equivalent terms are found in the same period, though it is more difficult to place them exactly; in French the corresponding terms appeared rather later. It is interesting that "con-scious" whose Latin source had meant "to know with" (to share knowledge with another), now came to mean "to know in oneself, alone." In seventeenth-century Europe *Homo sapiens* (the individual) had become so vividly aware of himself as a feeling, perceiving, and thinking person that in Germany and England, at least, he could no longer do without a term for it, a single word expressly referring to this experience.

This moment in the history of European languages marks a decisive phase in the social development of man. From this time onward the highest organic ordering processes in man tended increasingly to take the form either of the individual seeking to impose his personally preferred form of order on the disorder around him, or of the individual seeking to discover a form of order in himself which could survive in isolation from the environment.

The mystics represented, in extreme form, this second path of renunciation, the aim of which was to find a divine harmony in the soul by withdrawal and denial of the impatient demands of the self-conscious ego. The embarrassments of self-consciousness were to be cured by forgetting the self and developing an awareness of the divine. This path had a great appeal for some, in the West as in the East, but generally adopted it would lead to race suicide, and even for individuals it involves a shirking of the primary task: the maturing of the mind so that self-awareness is not denied, but used appropriately.

The rationalists, sustained by a mystical belief in conscious logic, adopted a response at the other extreme, seeking to impose their own order on experience and impatiently assuming that *the necessary principles or ideas were already available*. But they were not. The rationalists' conception of the skeptical consciousness or intellectual reason as the primary agent of the advancing human mind was wrong, as is now amply evident.

The remainder, constituting the majority of ordinary Europeans, perhaps less sensitive and less shocked by the contrast of the desire for order and the disorder of human life, took things more calmly and went about their business without assuming, as did both the mystics and the rationalists, that the answer was in principle already available, either as divine harmony or as conscious reason.

Of these three groups it was the rationalists who represented the spearhead of social advance. Their mistakes were the inevitable products of a transition toward a more mature and balanced view of man. The confusions of philosophy and the misuses of science are trivial beside this fact: the development of exact science is the sole unquestionably cumulative achievement of the human mind. But the rational intellect which claimed to be creating science was not the active principle behind its development.

Confronted by a universe in which neither order nor disorder prevails to the exclusion of the other, those whose faculties lay in the realm of speculative reason unconsciously sought to compensate the pain of their awareness of disorder by the search for general ideas which might reveal an underlying order and bring comfort. Here Plato had already marked out the way. This search for intellectual harmony is not, at root, a deliberate attempt to impose a fictitious order on a mainly disordered universe but a valid organic response: a movement to adjust the otherwise unbalanced judgment of human self-consciousness. Our attention and our faculty for direct experience is primarily drawn to contrast, clash, pain, disaster; the ordering tendency of the mind compensates this by leading us to recognize by inference the astonishingly powerful rules of ordering that prevail over great regions: for example, Newtonian gravitation, atomic theory, and the still unidentified principle of coordination which governs biological transformations. The impulse of intellectual reason to order the universe is a biologically authentic process, philosophically justified by its self-correcting character. "Reason," understood as the servant of deeper impulses, is the most reliable instrument yet available. As Hume [7] said, "Reason is, and ought only to be, the slave of the passions, and can never pretend to any other office than to serve and obey them," and beneath the "passions" must lie a biological principle of coordination.

But the self-correcting character of reason is only reliable tomorrow, never today—in the long run, never *now*. In any individual mind at any particular moment, or in any recorded analysis, reason is always somewhere at fault (though this fact may not matter for the point at issue). Reason can never know the hidden assumptions which restrict its momentary reasoning; no rational system—logical, mathematical, or scientific—can ever be used to define its own boundaries. For that the implicit assumptions must be made explicit in terms of a wider vision of possibilities. This will remain true until reason can create for itself a closed system which reveals limits inherent in the character of reason itself, for example, as an organic and historical theory of reason might make clear its necessary restrictions in man. This would imply that reason has to be regarded, not as primary, but as one expression of the ordering transformations of organic nature. However this possibility need not trouble anyone now, for any such closed theory lies far ahead.

The awkward fact—that reason, as we know it, is never

aware of its own hidden assumptions—has been too much for some philosophers, and even for many scientists to admit. Few have stated explicitly that their ideas were not correct, but merely the best available; that the greatest possible achievement of a single human mind, including their own, is to eliminate a few errors, while remaining blind to others.

This masculine kind of dogmatic abstract reasoning usually overreaches itself, thinks itself mature, and falls into the trap. Self-conscious man cannot use *conscious reason* to overcome his own impatience; for that he must surrender his conviction of the supreme importance of his own awareness and of the maturity of his reasoning; only if he can do that is he saved from humiliation. He must take his self-awareness with a little irony.

This is not easy. The pathology of the overemphasis of self-consciousness has increasingly affected the entire Western community over three centuries, and lies deep in social and individual habits. Hence the appeal of an equally pathological collectivism, and the emphasis on doctrines and groups. The frail awareness seeks comfort in conformity.

Many of the distresses of our age are due to the impatience of self-conscious man in treating his own personally preferred ideas, or conception of order, as final and universal. The psychological pressure to discover a compensating order leaves him no peace. "If the valid order is one I cannot yet recognize, what use is that to me? I cannot live by faith in an unknown order; I prefer my own. It at least expresses my convictions, serves my will, and solaces my pain, here and now."

Moreover, this habit of self-conscious man, to treat his own basic conceptions as final, was rendered the more intractable by their static character. As we have seen, the first ideas of the human mind, which were clear enough to permit any degree of systematization of contrasts, were representations of invariant aspects of experience. The mental traces of memory render permanent isolable aspects of experience; that which can be repeatedly isolated must in some sense be recurrent or persistent; the simplest kind of persistence is static invariance; hence the clearest unit ideas express such invariance; the mind has to develop far before it can master processes in which transformation plays as important a role as any invariant aspects. The temptation to treat static ideas as absolute, rather than partial and provisional, proved irresistible for many Western thinkers; the apparent clarity of such ideas seduces the mind into dismissing change or transformation as a trivial secondary effect of interactions between the "real" entities. Static concepts proved to be very effective intellectual tranquilizers; they enabled many thinkers for several centuries to continue at work, because they drugged the mind, inhibiting excessive awareness of the uncomfortably pervasive fact of change by drawing the attention elsewhere.

However intellectually convenient for contemporary specialist purposes—such as logical analysis, physical theory, and parts of biological theory (isolated unit genes, etc.)—this drugging is philosophically shocking, for it has temporarily blinded the human mind to one of the deepest intellectual problems: the interplay of constancy and change, wherever change is more than mere movement. Exact thinkers took up the study of constancy, and the study of change was left to those who accepted the immediacy of change, and these usually lacked even the desire for rational precision.

Heraclitus, with his followers in many fields, maintained the obvious but intellectually embarrassing principle of the primacy of change in the given world. But most systematic thinkers did not care to admit that, drugged by tranquilizers, they had been led into a philosophical ravine that must, sooner or later, prove to be a dead end.

Some recognized this situation early, though they could not estimate the importance which it possesses for us. Descartes' daring claim of clarity and simplicity made the danger evident to a few thinkers in the eighteenth century. One of the first was Diderot [8] who, in 1759, wrote of the "sophism of the ephemeral," "the sophism of a transient being who believes in the immortality of things."

Thus it came about that during the period after 1600, when the basis of rationalism was being laid, all the most powerful ideas were static. They did not involve any element of fundamental transformation and could be defined without using the conception of one-way temporal succession. The relation of *later than* played no part in ideas such as an eternal *God*, persisting *atoms* or other material entities, and the *soul* of the subject.

Yet in all personal experience and most observations of the world there is continual transformation from earlier to characteristically distinct later states. Static concepts are abstract, in the sense of neglecting a widespread, if not universal, feature of the given. Thus all the basic ideas of self-conscious man around 1600–1700 were abstractions achieved by emphasizing *permanent entities* and neglecting their changing relationships. In this manner transformation was apparently reduced to permanence.

This overemphasis on temporal invariance was inevitable at that time and would have been less harmful had it not been widely assumed that contemporary ideas and ideals were final. Minor discoveries of course remained to be made, but the main principles were correct—so it was assumed. And one of the deepest unquestioned assumptions, all the more powerful because deeply rooted in the unconscious habits of the Western mind, was this preference for static concepts. It was only because men gradually became aware of this preference and began to question it in many fields that the overemphasis on the self-consciousness of the permanent subject was, as we shall see, so swiftly corrected by the discovery of unconscious processes.

We here reach one of the most important developments in the history of the human mind, shown in the lower part of Chart A and in Chart B. *In Europe from around 1750 onward a shift of emphasis is evident in philosophical and scientific thought from static toward process concepts which is still in progress today.* Since this continuing movement is rendering the human intellect more powerful and extending its scope into new realms I shall call it *the great transformation.* Until now this change is one of emphasis only, for though it has affected thought in nearly all realms no one has yet shown how to construct a fundamental concept of "transformation" in which new entities or arrangements come into being and disappear.

The transformation from 1750 onward found its best known expression in the development of evolutionary ideas, but it coincided closely with the progressive recognition of unconscious mental processes. Darwin and Freud are at once products and promoters of the transformation. By showing that organic species and individual minds are fundamentally modified by the processes in which they partake, these two thinkers carried on the transformation of thought which had already begun. Yet their historical roles are sharply contrasted: Darwin presumably knew he was extending the scope of reason by helping to make it less static; it seems that Freud did not realize that he was destroying rationalism by showing that reason, though essential to understanding, did not control thought or behavior. But that is anticipating. Their main explicit influence on the structure of our thinking was as unconscious instruments of an intellectual transformation of whose historical extent and philosophical significance neither had an adequate conception. However, such awareness cannot be expected of minds formed in the nineteenth century, which lacked our own intense self-reflective thinking about thinking, that is, about the historical sources and the logical assumptions on which our thought is based.

As yet no general survey of the great transformation is available and a brief summary must therefore be given here to enable our story, which is one of its expressions, to be understood. For convenience in presentation I shall separate the inseparable and consider in turn four realms of scholarship: history; philosophy and psychology; biology; and finally physics, though so far it hardly merits mention here, except as an absentee. The transformation in three of these realms is shown in Chart B.

1. The prevalent interpretation of *human history* as a continuing sequence of changes set within the history of the evolution of species, of the solar system, and of the earth, rather than as the expression of a divine purpose which determines its significance and may at moments override its historical character, is first clearly evident in the seventeenth and eighteenth centuries. This historical outlook was strengthened during the seventeenth century by the recognition of the cumulative character of the new scientific discoveries and their irreversible effect on human society, by Descartes' cosmogony, and in the last decades of the century by geological discoveries. Between 1650 and 1750 scientists were becoming interested in the development of the physical universe, and there was a dim sense of the need for a valid concept of "development." One of the first historians to be influenced by this new attitude and to apply it in a philosophy of human history was Vico, who gave in his *New Science* (1723, 1742) a speculative picture of the earliest history of primitive mankind, though he introduced the idea of recurrence into the subsequent history of civilized man. During the second half of the century this historical attitude was matured by many

thinkers: Voltaire, Lessing, Kant, Herder, Schiller, Gibbon, and others, to become by the opening decades of the nineteenth century the dominant assumption of most historians. (The alternative interpretation, based on recurrent cycles within an eternal divine dispensation, has still been used, for example by Toynbee.)

2. In *philosophy and psychology* a parallel tendency is evident in the same period. The basically static outlook of Descartes (1596–1650)—except in his cosmogony— and of Spinoza (1632–1677) was modified to take more account of change and development by Leibniz (1646–1716) and Kant (1724–1804). It was finally discarded by Herder (1744–1803) and later by Goethe, Fichte, Schelling, Hegel, Schopenhauer, and many others, in favor of a primary developmental principle: creativity, productive reason, organic growth, or will, either unconscious or conscious. By the early nineteenth century this developmental approach had become dominant both in German systematic philosophy and in the general background of English writing. A similar movement is particularly clear in one branch of psychology: the increasing attention paid after 1750 to the productive or imaginative aspects of human thinking, e.g., from Herder (c. 1778) to Wertheimer (1945).

3. A major factor behind this almost general tendency was the growing interest in *biology*, particularly in the growth of organisms and their history. The relatively static ideas of earlier biologists, for example that of persisting forms that undergo cycles, which culminated in Linnaeus' classification of species (c. 1736), were gradually modified between 1740 and 1760 by the writings of Buffon, Maupertuis, Diderot, and Wolff, in which evolutionary ideas appear clearly for the first time. These were later extended by Herder, Monboddo, Lamarck, Erasmus Darwin, Welles, and Matthew, and finally established by Charles Darwin and Wallace in the theory of natural selection as the cause of the evolution of species.

The history of the idea of organic evolution between 1740 and the *Origin of Species* (1859) has been treated by many writers. But it has not, I believe, been adequately stressed that this movement is one component, or expression, of a more general change: a shift toward greater power and generality in the structure of the basic concepts of the Western intellect, potentially affecting all realms of thought. Basically this change is from *symmetrical relations* (like *equal to;* if A is equal to B, then it follows that B is equal to A), toward *asymmetrical relations* (like *greater than;* if B is greater than A, then A cannot be greater than B). Change, in the fuller sense of transformation, implies that something apparently changes into a later something else, and involves the asymmetrical relation *later than.* The historical transformation of thought is thus from ideas based primarily on symmetrical to others based on asymmetrical relations. This is the key to many of the intellectual problems which have concerned the Western intellect from 1750 to 1950, and there still remains one door which it must open.

For the search for adequate conceptions of one-way change still continues, and its successful culmination would mark an important step in the realization of the rational potentialities of the human brain-mind. This does not imply a change in the rules of logic, but the application of logic to more powerful classes of relations exploited in more extensive concepts and principles. For the asymmetrical relations in question include as a special degenerate case, and can be used to define, the corresponding symmetrical ones. Nearly static systems can be treated as those in which the element of transformation is negligible, but transformation is not, and cannot be represented as a special case of static invariance. Thus the great transformation is toward enlarged intellectual scope.

The simultaneity and close connections between these three movements in history, philosophy, and biology might suggest that they were aspects of a single trend producing a simultaneous effect in all realms of thought. But this is not the case, at least so far. The branch of thought which has been more influential in molding thought than any other since Copernicus, Kepler, and Galileo—mathematical physics—has here been strangely stubborn. In physics, where the quantitative correlation of thought and fact has been taken as the overriding criterion, it seems that the *Zeitgeist* is not omnipotent. One must welcome this resistance to uniformity, even if it raises interesting unsolved problems, indeed because it does.

4. Fundamental physical theory is a laggard in respect to the two-hundred-year-old transformation in other fields. For what are still held to be good reasons physical theory has (until very recently) preferred to regard time invariants, such as mass, energy, or mass-energy, and stable particles, as "obviously" primary, and to admit one-way processes only in the realm, presumably secondary, of statistical aggregates moving toward equilibrium. (Einstein, in his two theories of relativity, sought to treat temporal relations as similar to spatial.) But the discovery of increasing numbers of unstable entities which behave as if they were "elementary particles" is forcing a reconsideration of the adequacy of certain principles of invariance and symmetry, and this may lead to a more general physics of one-way processes. It is conceivable that the great transformation of thought will find its conclusion and justification in a physical theory of one-way transformations.

A consideration of these four realms reinforces the observation already made: that *no clear fundamental idea of the essential character of transformation has yet been formulated in any branch of knowledge.* No general rule is known which tells us when and how new entities or arrangements appear or disappear. In this respect the world of transformation, after three and a half centuries of exact science, still lies beyond our rational understanding.

Striking facts may remain almost unnoticed for generation after generation, if only the mind has unconsciously become accustomed to them. This strange antithesis cries for attention: static ideas in a world of process! Yet no fundamental thinker has yet thought fit to tackle the problem of transformation; few have even seen the problem clearly. But at a less fundamental level it was, as we have seen, precisely this antithesis that initiated the transformation around 1750: the contrast of observed processes to the static abstractions of the mathematics and physics of the period. At that time renewed attention to personal experience, to direct observations in many fields, and to the unchallengeable geological, archeological, and other records of the human and biological past, led many thinkers to the conclusion that change is a primary and pervasive feature of the world, and that the current mathematical and physical conceptions were idealized simplifying abstractions, powerful within their proper realms, but nonetheless partial and damaging since they drew attention away from the immediate and almost universal fact of change. This recognition is evident in many writers around 1750: Buffon, Diderot, Rousseau, and Hamann illustrate it in different contexts. Certainly no one school can claim a monopoly of this potentially universal appreciation, which was the prime source of the transformation.

A reasonably balanced and many-sided recognition of the inescapable immediacy of change, in contrast to the imposing static abstractions of exact reason, was first expressed by Herder (c. 1780). Nearly two centuries have passed, yet his brilliant though vague and emotional intuitions have not yet been replaced by an objective developmental doctrine applicable in all realms. Both Marx and Freud seemed to be aiming at this, each in his own sphere, but neither possessed an adequate understanding of the fundamental processes with which he was concerned, and each had to employ static abstractions which appear unsatisfactory today: separate, sup-posedly unchanging, economic classes; and persisting entities or regions (Superego, Ego, and Id) into which the mind is assumed to be divisible.

The transformation which I have here outlined was prob-ably the most important factor leading European thinkers after 1800 to correct the overemphasis on consciousness. For the split of experience into subject and object had only suited the mind because both are relatively permanent, and both can be directly perceived as *objects* of perception or introspection, while the actual process of experiencing and of acquiring knowledge is transitory, obscure, and intangible. This might not have been so if man had possessed an organ which gave him direct perceptive awareness of the "body-mind" rela-tions, that is, of the actual processes, and not merely the re-sults, of perception, cognition, selection, judgment, and so on. But as things are, in the human brain's search for stable aspects of experience, the split into experiencing subject and external object was appropriate and in some sense unavoidable as a first step.

Any advance from this dualism was difficult until the trans-formation had begun to prepare the way. If change is nearly universal, and subject and object are not really permanent but merely changing components of a wider system itself undergoing continual transformations, if all cognition rests on interactions between subject and object—which change them—then it is clear that the next step should not be to isolate more powerful invariants, but to come to grips with the interactions viewed as a changing pattern of relations in the complete system: changing subject *plus* changing object, for while interacting both are subject to change.

The Cartesian split is inescapable while the demand is made for static concepts, unconsciously or consciously. On that basis static thought cannot improve on Descartes, the "body-mind relation" having remained almost as obscure in 1959 as it was in 1659, for lack of a clear concept of transformation. But once change is accepted as pervasive the problem can be restated, and new vistas may be opened to empirical and theoretical investigation. The subject of study becomes a one-way sequence of transformations, with some continuity of pattern but no invariant material identity (since even atoms come and go) and no invariant subjective identity (since growth, experience, and decline affect awareness irreversibly). When science has identified, perhaps many decades hence, the structural changes in the experiencing subject and the perceived object which correspond to the processes of experiencing, observing, and thinking, it is likely that the old problems of the body-mind relation will appear in a new light.

That culmination may lie far ahead. Certainly the first tentative efforts to correct the Cartesian assumptions began far in the past, even *before* the general transformation began around 1750. This was possible because some monistic religious thinkers did not take the static scientific concepts of the seventeenth century as seriously as others. For example, Christian theologians were among the first—after Descartes— to make explicit suggestions regarding the existence of what we now call unconscious mental processes.

But these early speculations, made within a religious context, had little influence. It is not the first expression or the earliest discovery of an idea within a particular community that counts, but the person who does it in a special historical context. Ten, perhaps a hundred, discoveries are made for every one which the community is ready to recognize. Originality is not uncommon and the community, as expressed through its corporate instruments, is always blind to the color of what is new. The array of early speculators, taken one by one, fascinating as they are, are only important for our story because very slowly, after two centuries, their cumulative efforts convinced the post-Cartesian dualists that their dichotomy of *res cogitans* and *res extensa* was of no further use in promoting clarity, the interactions which this dualism neglected having become more important than their apparent separation.

Indeed, looking back on the story, the most striking features of the historical correction of the Cartesian error are the swiftness with which it began in a few minds, and the slowness with which it reached the schools and the professions. Insights may be impulsive, but teaching must be conservative.

IV

The Discovery
of the Unconscious

SELF-CONSCIOUS MAN thinks he thinks. This has long been recognized to be an error, for the conscious subject who thinks he thinks is not the same as the organ which does the thinking. The conscious person is one component only, a series of transitory aspects, of the thinking person.

This misinterpretation led to extraordinary achievements and strange embarrassments. To the first because it gave the individual a sense of his independence, power, and responsibility; nothing was beyond him to learn; his conscious mind was primary and free, though perhaps lent to him by God. To the second because, as we have seen, this power and freedom of the conscious mind is partly illusory, the person being more than his immediate awareness.

There have probably been individuals in every culture who knew that factors of which we are not directly aware influence thought and behavior. As I have suggested, this recognition must have been widespread, for example in China where a more balanced and unified view of mind than that of Cartesian Europe was prevalent in some periods. And certainly in ancient Greece, in Rome, and through the centuries of the Middle Ages many thinkers, some of great influence, avoided the self-centered mistake of treating the awareness of the individual as primary in the realm either of value or of philosophical thought. For them the direct experiences of the person were subordinate to other principles, divine or material, that in some degree controlled the fate of the individual and influenced his awareness. This was indeed the almost universal assumption, explicit or concealed, until self-conscious Europeans began to treat mind as an autonomous realm of being, a thing following its own laws.

No thinker ever imagined that "body" and "mind"—insofar as the terms are valid—are without apparent interactions. We must leave it to the Cartesian scholars, as Descartes did, to explain what it meant to postulate, as one of the first products of clear thinking, two independent realms which are none the less so intimately interdependent. The lesson is that the more brilliant the light cast on two neighboring realms, the more profound the obscurity into which their interactions are thrown.

I use the term "discovery of the unconscious" not in the sense of a scientific discovery supported by systematic tests, but of a *new inference*, the bringing to light of what was previously unknown in a particular culture. The discovery of the unconscious was the spreading out of the intellectual illumination that Descartes had focused too sharply. This discovery was unnecessary before him; it was the prestige of Cartesian ideas that created the "problem of the unconscious."

During the late seventeenth century three main attitudes

dominated European philosophical thought, corresponding to three interpretations of the nature of existence. Material- ism treated physical bodies and their motions as the primary reality; idealism took it to be spirit or mind; while Cartesian dualism postulated two independent realms: the mental *res cogitans* and the material *res extensa*. For the first two schools there was no difficulty in recognizing unconscious mentality, though under other names. To the materialists all mentality was physiological, and the existence of unconscious physio- logical processes, similar to and influencing thought, was an immediate consequence of the fact that our direct awareness of the processes in our bodies is restricted. And to the ideal- ists all natural processes were the expression of a universal mind or world spirit of which the human individual has no direct knowledge, though it shares, in some degree, the char- acteristics of human mentality. Thus for the idealists also there was no problem; the unconscious mind of the individual was not in any way surprising; it was merely a part of the universal mind to which the individual awareness enjoyed no direct access. But to the third, Cartesian, school the ad- mission of the existence of unconscious mental processes pre- sented an acute philosophical challenge, for it demanded the discarding of the original conception of the dualism, as one of two independent realms, matter in motion and mind neces- sarily aware. For those who were loyal to Descartes, all that was not conscious in man was material and physiological, and therefore not mental.

If the three schools had enjoyed equal authority there would have been no intellectual difficulty or historical drama in the recognition of the unconscious, for the monists would have achieved it without any disturbance, as indeed several did. *But no monism, whether mystical, religious, or scientific, has yet provided a sufficiently lucid and stable basis for the progressive clarification of thought covering both realms. As* we have seen, the cerebral preference for static concepts made dualism or pluralism necessary as a first step, if the complexity of experience is to be reflected. Thus the Cartesian dualism corresponded to a deep tendency in the human mind; what it did was to express that tendency for the first time in systematic form. Neither the Christian idealistic nor the scientific physiological monists could offer a satisfying alternative to the dualism, and from that time onward behind the disputes of the academies Europeans did most of their thinking in terms of the split. We still use the dualistic terms, though the separation has long been exposed as misleading.

Thus the situation displayed an unfortunate paradox: most thinking was based on error which ultimately would impede advance, but the two schools which were readiest to recognize the unconscious mind, and did in fact do so, could not contribute greatly to the advance, because their monisms were both relatively impotent: the idealists could not link their universal mind with physical phenomena, and physiologists were too ignorant (as they still are today) to know how to build the bridge from the other side by showing how their electrically pulsating cerebral tissues simulate mentality. The two schools for which there was in principle no difficulty could contribute nothing to the solution of a problem which thus became the embarrassing responsibility of the third: to break down the separation of the two realms, starting with a broader interpretation of mentality.

The issue can be interpreted as one of definition: no school knew how to define "mentality" so that understanding could best advance. The idealists postulated mind as primary, but did not understand it; the materialists had a reasonably good definition of matter, but could not use it to define mind; and the dualists, while claiming mind as one basic concept in a dualistic theory, continually shifted their ground in trying to explain what was meant by it. "Unconscious mental processes" sounds impressive, particularly if a clear meaning is given to the term "unconscious," which may not be too difficult. But what does "mental" mean? It is here that the problem lies. *No one yet knows how properly to define "mental,"* perhaps because this can only be done within a valid monism.

All that we know is that there are other processes or factors, in some respects so similar to conscious mentality that they can with justification also be called mental, which must be taken into account in understanding our minds and our behavior. The term "unconscious mental processes" is the enunciation of a program of research: to discover the true structure and function of mentality in terms of a single doctrine replacing the dualism which has broken down.

The discovery of the unconscious by self-conscious man occupied some two centuries, roughly from 1700 to 1900. As we shall see in the next chapters, *the idea of unconscious mental processes was, in many of its aspects, conceivable around 1700, topical around 1800, and became effective around 1900,* thanks to the imaginative efforts of a large number of individuals of varied interests in many lands. Opinions may differ regarding the relative importance of their thought and the extent to which they influenced each other. But research proves that more than fifty individuals in Germany, England, and France alone, whose works are easily accessible, contributed during the two hundred years from 1680 to 1880 to the creation of a steadily developing climate of thought regarding the unconscious mind, and that many of them made systematic introspective studies, laboratory experiments, and even clinical applications of the new idea. During these two centuries the *existence* of the unconscious mind was being established; the discovery of its *structure* only began in the twentieth century.

Several factors forced this development in thought and practice, but the most important, underlying all the others,

was the recognition—which even Descartes could not avoid—
that the facts do not support the assumption of the autonomy
of consciousness. In varying degrees representatives of nearly
all fields—religious, literary, philosophical, and scientific—
contributed to the growth of the idea of the unconscious
because it is an unavoidable inference from experience. No
one tradition enjoys a monopoly of fertile ideas; even the
exact sciences continually receive important suggestions from
the varied background of the cultural tradition. It was the
broad tradition of thought, as much as newly discovered facts,
that gradually forced the scientific specialists to be more receptive to the idea of the unconscious mind.

This pervasive pressure of old and new facts was strengthened by the general transformation of thought from 1750
onward, but it was expressed through certain channels which
directly encouraged speculations regarding the unconscious
mind:

1. The steady development of interest in the experiences
of the individual, evident from the eleventh century onward,
leading to two contrasted approaches: (a) the romantic and
transcendental philosophies toward the end of the eighteenth
century, and the German *Naturphilosophie* of 1800–1830;
and (b) the establishment of a science of the psychology of
the individual using scientific methods, from about 1800
onward.

2. The encouragement given by biological (genetic, developmental, and evolutionary) ideas to greater emphasis on
vitality, organic tendencies, and will, as a background to the
reasoning intellect.

3. The impact of ideas from other, mainly Eastern, traditions which placed greater emphasis on feeling and emotion
and had never attempted to separate the conscious mind
from other phenomena in the radical manner of the Cartesians. Ideas from India and China, in particular, began

noticeably to influence European thinking during the eighteenth century.

These related influences together created an irresistible pressure: the romantics needed the unconscious as a link with universal powers, the psychologists as a continuity behind the transient moments of awareness, the biologists provided the vital background of organic will and unconscious motive, and Eastern thought the sense of a pervasive unity of which the individual was a part.

Post-Cartesian speculations regarding unconscious mentality had begun before 1700, but from 1750 onward these combined influences began to produce a fresh orientation of thought. We are here mainly concerned with systematic verbal formulations, and in this respect the German language contribution was the most important. Those who trust national generalizations may consider that this was due to the fact that many German thinkers at that time were *par excellence* theorizers, concerned with the universal application of a very few ideas. Or possibly to a German Protestant tendency toward personal culture and an *Innerlichkeit* involving an introspective isolation of the individual. This was in contrast to the French complementary emphasis on a civilized society and to the English more empirical, practical, and political tradition. Whether valid or not these interpretations are not fundamental, for no philosophy of history tells us either when and why such national characteristics developed, or how permanent they are.

However that may be, the history of the rise of self-conscious man and of the discovery of the unconscious after Descartes shows a dominant German contribution in the realm of systematic ideas, English support on the empirical side, and French verbal caution combined with intuitive subtlety. The German language tradition certainly displays most evidence both of an occasional intellectual obsession

with the self-awareness of the individual, and later of a need
to correct this by substituting, not a more balanced personal
attitude, but a better theory of the mind. The most representative and influential figures in the expression of the discovery of the unconscious in explicit formulations were
German-speaking. But we must not forget the immeasurable
influence of Shakespeare and Rousseau; the fertile interactions
of varied traditions, within and outside Europe; and the part
played by thinkers in smaller communities.

One generalization is safe: the French, under the combined
influence of Catholicism and of Descartes, played a relatively
small role in the explicit development of the idea of the unconscious mind, compared with either the German or the
English. The English contribution is less known, except to
specialists, but it was early and of great importance. On the
other hand, in spite of one or two notable names and the great
influence of French psychiatry, with its interest in hypnotism
and hysteria from Mesmer to Charcot, French minds contributed relatively little to theoretical understanding of the processes involved.

In language the true units of meaning may be phrases
rather than single words, and some communities may have a
weakness, and others a dislike, for inventing new words. Nonetheless the first usage of a word in any language marks a significant moment in the development of religious, philosophical, or scientific ideas. The available surveys suggest that
Unbewusstsein and *bewusstlos* (in meanings close to those
now current) were first used by E. Platner in 1776, and these
or similar terms were made popular by Goethe, Schiller, and
Schelling between 1780 and 1820. The word "unconscious"
as an adjective (with the same meaning) appears in English
in 1751, and more frequently after 1800, for example, in the
writings of Wordsworth and Coleridge. By 1850 both adjective and noun were extensively used in Germany, and were
moderately common in England.

But in France *inconscient,* as adjective or noun, was probably not used until the 1850's, and then mainly in translating the German terms. Amiel, who read German extensively, speaks of *la vie inconsciente* (in relation to man) around 1860, and earlier usages must have been few. A French dictionary published in 1862 includes *inconscient* as "very rarely used," and the conservative *Dictionnaire de l'Académie Française* only admitted the word in 1878. French was in this respect half a century behind both German and English.

If we turn to consider the main sequence of European thought as represented in its leading thinkers we find that in the post-Cartesian period increasing attention was paid to different aspects of unconscious mental processes, roughly in the following sequence:

memory;
perception;
ideas;
instinct, vitality, will, imagination;
dreams, pathology;
therapeutic applications.

Unconscious memory, perception, and ideas were considered very early, and the speculation regarding therapeutic applications came rather late. But there are exceptions to this general sequence. All that it is safe to conclude is that between 1680 and 1880 a large number of thinkers, some of them with little apparent influence, considered one or more of the following aspects of unconscious mental processes:

memory, and its pathology;
perception, images, ideas;
reasoning, inference;
selection, judgment, diagnosis;
imagination, invention, creation, inspiration;
ecstasies, premonitions, visions;
vital impulses, volition, motive, interest, sympathy, aversion, falling in love;

conflict, inhibition, dissociation, hysteria, obsession, per-
versions;

mental therapeutics for physical and mental pathology;

dreams, hallucinations, somnambulism, suggestion, hypnotism;

alcohol, drugs. diseases;

collective myths, religions;

personal and social rationalizations.

No one considered all known aspects in a scientific and
comprehensive manner. Freud neglected one of the most important, had nothing fresh to say about it, and seems only
to have occasionally mentioned it in passing: the general
character of the unconscious mental processes which underlie
the appearance of novelty in all creation, imagination, and
invention. On this primary characteristic of unconscious processes he remained almost silent.

As we shall see, each of these aspects was considered by
several writers before 1850, a number of them before 1750. If
an idea of this depth and revolutionary significance was to
become socially effective by, say, 1920, it is not surprising to
find that many aspects of it were conceivable around 1700
and topical by 1800. Allowing for human conservatism in relation to everything that lies deep, twenty decades or eight
generations is not long for the idea of the unconscious to
have attained partial maturity and produced social changes.

It has been argued by Lovejoy [9] that the Western "revolt
from psychophysical dualism" and the "dethronement of
Descartes" took place mainly during the present century, between 1900 and 1930. This may be true of academic thought
in a narrow context, but it implies too restricted a view of
the history and interactions of ideas. We have seen that the
revolt began at once, in the same century as Descartes, but
that it has developed slowly for lack of any clear monistic
ideas fit to be substituted. As I have said, within this varied

movement and underlying all its special expressions lay one
primary factor: the facts. But this must be seen in a broad
context. It was the facts, not merely as observed, but also as
experienced, and the basis of the human response to them
was not merely the intellectual impulse to recognize a rational order in phenomena, but this impulse serving as an
instrument to assist man, first in recognizing the potentialities of his own nature, and secondly in realizing them. Thus
the fundamental agent, the ultimate driving force, behind
the discovery of the unconscious was that element of surplus
vitality, or refusal to be content with life as it is, which had
the power to force self-conscious man to transcend his image
of himself, to become richer as a person by recognizing the
limitations of his current idea of himself. The movement
was more than a phase in intellectual history, it was a step
toward a more mature human life; not a return to a primitive unity, but a movement aiming at a differentiated ordering of life sustained by a more complete and objective knowledge of nature and human nature. Historically, as these three
centuries moved through their course, what was developing
seemed to be *Rousseau plus Newton,* emotional unreason
plus quantitative science. We may hope that it can be better
understood as a transition through the disharmonies of Rousseau, Newton, and Freud, toward a better adapted mode of
thinking and of spontaneity which lacks, as yet, a representative name—possibly a *Goethe* less self-oriented and supported
by more comprehensive and cautious sciences of nature and
man, an enriched humanism.

The core of the discovery certainly lay where the transitional disease of rationalistic self-consciousness accompanied
by reverence for human creativity was most intense: in Germany. It is in the Romantic movement there, influenced by
Shakespeare and Rousseau, that we find the earliest focus of
the new idea, from which all its special expressions flow: the

valid principle that in the unconscious mind lies the contact of the individual with the universal powers of nature. The springs of human nature lie in the unconscious, for it links the individual with the universal, or at least the organic. This is true, whether it is expressed as the union of the soul with the divine, or as the realm which links the moments of human awareness with the background of organic processes within which they emerge. But the fascination of the idea arises because it is felt to be the source of power, the home of the *élan* which moves us, the active principle which leads us to feel, to imagine, to judge, to think, and to act. This is more than mechanics, or dynamics, or chance; it is a principle of biological surplus vigor, of potential order or organization continually coming into being as far as clash permits.

It is therefore not surprising that we find a complementary tendency in Europeans during the period of self-conscious man, indeed at the very moment when self-awareness was being widely acclaimed as primary in theory and value, leading them to pay increased attention to what appear to ordinary waking consciousness as less normal or pathological states. From the eighteenth century onward growing interest was shown not only in the normal rhythms of consciousness (sleep, dreams, reveries, etc.), but also in unusual or pathological states (fainting, ecstasy, hypnosis, hallucinations, dissociation, drugged conditions, epilepsy, forgetfulness, etc.) and in processes underlying ordinary thought (imagination, judgment, selection, diagnosis, interest, sympathy, etc.).

It seemed to self-conscious man that many of these phenomena lay in a realm of the "irrational" challenging that of the "rational" where he believed himself to be at home. This was a mistake, based on his misunderstanding and exaggeration of the role of "reason," as can be seen at many levels of analysis. First, there are no separable realms: all sustained mental processes, including those into which awareness enters

temporarily, are primarily unconscious, and are largely guided
by unconscious factors. Second, there is no reason to regard
unconscious processes as intrinsically irrational (in the sense
of contrary or antagonistic to rational analysis or behavior),
merely because we do not yet understand the organization
and operation of the mind, or because they may acquire a
pathological disorder. This sense of an antagonism between
conscious reason and unconscious mental processes arises only
in the dissociated mind. It is certainly obvious enough, thanks
to Freud, that unconscious factors can (e.g., where there is
repression, dissociation, and deformation) lead to behavior
contrary to reason, but that is no ground for misrepresenting
the operations of the unconscious imagination and judgment
as always unreasonable, for they provide the basis for rational
thought. It is reason which must grow more comprehensive
so that it can understand, assist, and fuse with—though it
will never replace—the ordering processes of the unconscious.
The discovery of the unconscious is the recognition of a
Goethean order, as much as of a Freudian disorder, in the
depths of the mind.

But for two centuries, say from 1750 to 1950, many rationalists tended to regard the unconscious as the realm of
irrational forces threatening the social and intellectual order
which the rational consciousness, they imagined, had built up
over generations. Day was challenged by Night, the enlightenment of reason by the tempests and conflicts of intuition
and instinct, the soul of man by a dark and frightening, but
desperately attractive, inner spirit of temptation and surrender, ready to take over and bring the peace of self-
forgetfulness. Night, dream, self-annihilation in the abysses of
sensuality, escape from the pretenses of the social and intellectual life to a sincere and spontaneous acceptance of the
depths. But this attraction of the dark was merely the reverse
side of the pretense that man had already discovered the

light: the ideals and ideas, Platonic or Christian, religious or rational, appropriate to his nature. For others who saw deeper the unconscious was not a realm merely of chaos, conflict, and destructive passions, but the source also of all the forms of order created by the human imagination since man's first and most extraordinary formative achievement: the development of language. Thus we can, to some extent at least, see in each of the contrasted concepts of the unconscious the expression of a corresponding type of human temperament:

The Unconscious Mind Was Interpreted

By:	As:
Mystics	The link with God
Christian Platonists	A divine, universal, plastic principle
Romantics	The link between the individual and universal powers
Early Rationalists	A factor operating mainly in memory, perception, and ideas
Post-Romantic Thinkers	Organic vitality, expressed in will, imagination, and creation
Dissociated "Self-Conscious Man"	Night: the realm of violence
Physical Scientists	The consequence of physiological factors not yet understood
Monistic Thinkers	The prime mover and source of all order and novelty in thought and action

Freud ("Subconscious")	Mainly inhibited memories ruled by the pleasure principle, in a state of deformation and conflict, accessible only through special techniques; also forgotten memories and inaccessible levels
Jung	The prerational realm of collective myth and religious symbolisms

Yet to separate too sharply these contrasted conceptions is to misunderstand them. The mystic believes in an unknown God, the thinker and scientist in an unknown order; it is hard to say which surpasses the other in nonrational devotion. But while the mystic retreats, the scientist goes out to explore. To interpret the unconscious mind as the link with God is to invite a surrender to ignorance, unless it is coupled with curiosity about things as they are. And we shall see that the first European (known to me) who, after Descartes, gave an interesting sketch of some of the activities of the unconscious mind in health was, most appropriately, a Christian monist interested in science.

The advance from the naïve overemphasis of consciousness toward a balanced scientific understanding of the unconscious, perhaps still some generations ahead, has been so far mainly the result, first of speculative philosophical thought, and later of the clinical and laboratory study of personality and behavior, the study of the physiology of the central nervous system and brain having as yet contributed relatively little. Our detailed understanding of the over-all organization of the processes of the central nervous system and of the mode of operation of the (animal or human) brain as a selecting, recording, ordering, and controlling organ has not advanced greatly in the last few decades, relative to its importance. Thus unless a further physiological clarification is achieved soon, the twenty-first century may be opening before the neurophysiology of the brain and the psychology of the mind are replaced by a single doctrine of the coordinated structure and processes of the human organ of thought.

However, the application of the growing understanding of unconscious mental processes to human therapy began many decades ago and has achieved much, though hindered by the still partial character of theoretical knowledge. The ancients used drugs and rituals to cure mental disease, but the idea of applying the developing objective knowledge of unconscious processes to provide techniques for treating pathological mental conditions first appeared around the end of the eighteenth century, and the first systematic professional efforts to base curative procedures on theories of the structure of unconscious mental processes were made a hundred years later, in the last decades of the nineteenth century. Measured against the importance of such knowledge and techniques, the fifty years and more which have passed since these attempts began, and the high hopes placed on them, it is unfortunate that no self-improving *psychological* methods of permanently curing grave mental conditions have yet been established. Freud did not regard the benefits of psychoanalysis to the neurotic individual or even to the analyzed analyst as normally complete or permanent, and his own techniques have not yet led to important discoveries improving and extending them. His contribution, as far as one can judge twenty years after his death, has been more to social, professional, and parental *understanding* than to wholly satisfactory techniques for therapy. Certainly theoretical insight was his chief personal concern. He was as optimistic regarding the possibility of discovering the laws of the psyche as he was pessimistic regarding the prospect of that moral improvement which he regarded as the *desideratum* in the individual and in society. Here the contrast provided by the physical approach is striking. Since 1920 important cumulative advances have been made in the physical treatment of certain psychoses, though they have not been based on any theoretical understanding, physiological or psychological, of the reasons for their success.

Thus the century has so far achieved partial understanding of the mind, in the form mainly of a dramatized allegory —the Freudian doctrine with its recent variants—and has made widely available a miscellaneous array of methods of treatment, from confessional and analysis to drugs and shock. If the whole field of the understanding and treatment of the human thinking organ is taken into account there have been minor but definite advances in nearly every decade since 1900. Yet the situation remains confused. There is no uniting humane philosophy, no comprehensive scientific theory, no satisfying order in what is known. And a great deal is still unknown.

This situation might be an unavoidable consequence of the fact that here science confronts the secrets of the subject—a part of the human mind seeking to understand the whole— and this task might conceivably lie beyond the scope of the self-checking interplay of theory and observation which we call science. But there is no compelling reason yet to assume this, though it may be necessary for science to change its concepts and to broaden its methods.

Having regard to the achievements of the various scientific methods, it is more probable that the present theoretical confusion and therapeutic uncertainty (in some realms) is transitory, the existence of the unconscious mind having become clear, but its basic structure and mode of operation being still obscure. This distinction is sometimes forgotten. The physicists discovered the nucleus of the atom fifty years ago and they have recently learned how to exploit its internal energy. But they do not yet understand the laws of its structure. The recognition of the existence of a class of phenomena is different from the identification of the laws they obey. Yet to name a thing is an important step, for it suggests the task of finding an appropriate definition, and that leads in turn to the attempt to discover its characteristic form of order, its way of working.

V

The Discoverers:
Before 1730

As Margetts [10] has said, "Almost since the dawn of civilization man has had an inkling of understanding that mind activity outside of our waking consciousness does exist." This could be proved by citations from the Indian Upanishads, from ancient Egypt and Greece, and, I believe, from many other civilizations. All the greatest human documents, such as the Old and New Testaments and the writings of Plato, Dante, Cervantes, and Shakespeare, reveal this understanding.

In the present and subsequent chapters we salute some of the more accessible writers in our own culture who have shown this awareness. But we should not forget that there must have been a vastly greater number who shared this realization without recording their thoughts. Moreover we are not concerned with "first" expressions of any idea—that often

77

U.B.F.— G

has no clear meaning and cannot be determined—but only with early examples, mainly in post-Cartesian Europe.

One of the attractions of this survey is that it is necessary to neglect most of the distinctions between one thinker and another which are indispensable for other scholarly purposes, and to pass freely from mystic to scientist, from poet to philosopher, and even from dualist to monist, in tracing a nearly universal developing awareness. We are here following a complex idea in course of growth through decades and centuries. The quotations * are designed to illustrate this, and must not be taken to represent adequately their author's point of view. They are torn from context and should, as far as possible, be given the meanings which they had for their author.

The chief lesson of this study lies in the fact that it can never be complete. A few hours of additional search and another forgotten figure comes to light who had his own inkling of an understanding of our idea. In other peoples and languages there are certainly many further examples bearing on our theme. For there are as many different approaches to it as there are kinds of human temperament.

Every rule must be broken and though our story begins after 1637 it cannot be understood without a few reminders of what had already been thought in earlier times.

Those who are in earnest in the search for reliable knowledge even if the race has to wait long for it, will appreciate why I choose the first experimental physiologist to open the sequence of discoverers:

Galen (c. A.D. 130–200), Greek physician and founder of experimental physiology, is credited with the recognition that we make unconscious inferences from perceptions. This initiates the story appropriately, since the conception of unconscious mental processes was itself born as an unconscious inference from external or internal perceptions, and experi-

* For sources of quotations in Chapters V–VIII see *References* at end of book.

mental physiology has still to make a decisive contribution to our theme.

It is equally fitting to pass at once to a Neoplatonic thinker: *Plotinus* (c. 204–270), a philosopher who spent the last thirty years of his life in Rome. He suggested that we only become aware of the processes of thought when we pay attention to them:

[Just as a mirror correctly placed provides an image, but when displaced fails to reflect the continuing process] so when the analogous feature [mirror] is present in the soul, wherein the images of reflection and of the mind are mirrored, these latter are seen and the higher recognition is present that the mind and soul are active. But when this [the mirror in us] is broken, on account of the disturbed harmony of the organism, then the mind and soul think without the mirror image, and then thought is present without an inner image of itself.

Feelings can be present without awareness of them.

The absence of a conscious perception is no proof of the absence of mental activity.

St. Augustine (354–430), the great Christian philosopher, was deeply impressed, as Plato had been, by the power of memory.

Great is this power of memory, exceedingly great. O my God, a spreading limitless room within me. Who can reach its uttermost depth? Yet it is a faculty of soul and belongs to my nature. In fact I cannot totally grasp all that I am. Thus the mind is not large enough to contain itself: but where can that part of it be which it does not contain? Is it outside itself and not within? How can it not contain itself? As this question struck me, I was overcome with wonder and almost stupor. Here are men going afar to marvel at the heights of mountains, the mighty waves of the sea, the long courses of great rivers, the vastness of the ocean, the movements of the stars, yet leaving themselves unnoticed . . .

St. Thomas Aquinas (1224–1274) developed a systematic theory of the mind, stressing in particular the body-mind unity, and the importance of unconscious features:

I do not observe my soul apart from its acts. There are thus processes in the soul of which we are not immediately aware.

It was an essential feature of the mystical tradition that the most important insights are not gained by the deliberate pursuit of knowledge, but by what Keats called the "negative capability," or ability to make oneself empty and to receive. Hence a saying attributed to *Dionysius Areopagiticus* (? c. A.D. 50):

The most godly knowledge of God is that which is known by unknowing.

This feature of mystical thought runs through the centuries to Jakob Boehme, Schelling, Schopenhauer, and Nietzsche, and contributed much to the background of our story. Thus *Meister Eckhart* (?–1327), the German mystical philosopher, says:

A really perfect person will be so dead to self, so lost in God, so given over to the will of God, that his whole happiness consists in being unconscious of self and its concerns, and being conscious instead of God.

Writing of the thirteenth century Vyvyan [11] has suggested, with *Le Roman de la Rose* in mind, that "a psychoanalytical technique was then being used [in medieval poetry] for artistic creation as consciously as the psychiatrist uses one today for the healing of a neurosis." Here Vyvyan is referring to the dual role of figures in a story: as persons in their own right and as projections of largely unconscious aspects of a central figure.

This early awareness was not restricted to general aspects of the unconscious; it extended even to the psychopathology of everyday life, as, for example, in the tricks of memory.

Dante (1265–1321) knew that shameful memories are often forgotten. In the *Purgatorio* Dante and Beatrice are in conversation:

> Therefore I answered: "I remember not
> That ever I estranged myself from thee
> Nor there-in does my conscience bring remorse."
> "If now thou hast no memory thereof,"
> Smiling she answered me, "Recall to mind
> How thou of Lethe e'en this day didst drink.
> As from the smoke the fire may be inferred,
> So thy forgetfulness doth clearly prove,
> Fault in thy will, that otherwhere was bent."

Paracelsus (1493–1541), Swiss physician, represents a transition between the mystical and the scientific attitudes. Many of his ideas imply that there are influences, at once biological and spiritual, guiding man of which he is seldom aware. C. G. Jung says, "Of all Paracelsus' intuitions the Aquaster comes nearest to the modern conception of the Unconscious." For Paracelsus the imagination is creative power and takes precedence over all other faculties. In this he was followed by Boehme, and later by many poets and philosophers. Paracelsus also recognized the part played by mind in disease.

It is fitting, perhaps, that one of the most penetrating descriptions of the mystical path was written just before modern science was born, and yet contains passages which read like a moralist's defense of psychoanalysis:

Of these the first benefit is the knowledge of the self and its own vileness. . . . Hereby the soul learns the reality of its own misery, which before it knew not. . . . Other benefits . . . flow as from their proper source and fount, that of self-knowledge.

This is from *St. John of the Cross* (1542–1591), Spanish mystic, in *The Dark Night of the Soul*. It leads us to *Jakob Boehme* (1575–1642), German shoemaker and one of the greatest mystics, for whom an unconscious will was the source of everything, divine and natural:

Before God I do not know how the thing arises in me, without the participation of my will. I do not know that which I must write.

For Boehme "the hidden man is God's own being," and as for many after him, including Jung, God is found "underneath" rather than "above." God is the spring, the root, the "abyss." Nature rises out of God, and we sink into Him. God is nature.

Boehme's importance cannot be measured. Hegel called him "the father of German philosophy," and Schopenhauer, who owed much to him, said that Schelling took the ideas of one of his works straight from Boehme. If he "lived and moved and had his being in God" it might equally be said that when he was not making shoes, he was exploring, by introspection, a unity hidden in his own nature beneath all conflict.

However none of these minds displays the confident spirit of inquiry, the combination of reverent inquisitiveness and scientific concentration, that marks a later period. In the ultimate analysis science is born of myth and religion, all three being expressions of the ordering spirit of the human mind. But it is only when the individual mind accepts its own authority as superior to the inherited tradition that this spirit becomes aware of itself and confident of its powers.

Montaigne (1532–1592) was one of the earliest to achieve this emancipation from medieval tradition. Here we are only concerned with the intimations in this skeptical mind of the limited role of awareness.

. . . So it happens to us in the yawning of sleep, before it has fully possessed us, to perceive, as in a dream, what is done about us, and to follow the last things that are said with a perplexed and uncertain hearing which seems but to touch the borders of the soul; and to make answers to the last words that have been spoken to us, which have more in them of chance than sense. Now seeing I have in effect tried it, I have no doubt but I have hitherto made a right judgment . . . for we have many motions in us that do not proceed from our direction; . . . so falling people extend their arms before them by a natural impulse, which prompts our limbs to offices and motions without any commission from our reason . . .

Now, those passions which only touch the outward bark of us, cannot be said to be ours: to make them so, there must be concurrence of the whole man; and the pains which are felt by the hand or the foot while we are sleeping, are none of ours . . .

In the following passage Montaigne describes his condition after an accident:

This consideration should seem to proceed from a soul that retained its functions: but it was nothing so with me. I knew not what I said or did, and they were nothing but idle thoughts in the clouds, that were stirred up by the senses of the eyes and ears, and

proceeded not from me. I knew not for all that, whence I came
or whither I went, neither was I capable to weigh and consider
what was said to me: these were light effects, that the senses produced of themselves as of custom; what the soul contributed was
in a dream, lightly touched, licked and bedewed by the soft
impression of the senses . . .

The name of *Cervantes* (1547–1616) is included here as a
reminder that there have been many writers with understanding of "depth psychology" who are not quoted in this survey
for lack of space or of scholarship, or because their insights
are left implicit and cannot be extracted in bits. Don Quixote
is a study of the growth, defense, wearing down, and collapse
of a delusion of consciousness. An undercurrent of doubt, of
repressed knowledge that it was all self-delusion, runs through
the story.

This is perhaps the place to apologize to the quoted authors
for tearing these pieces from their original context. But I
have placed them in a grander context of which any man may
be proud.

Shakespeare (1564–1616) reflects and strengthens the growing awareness of the depths of the mind. I have left these
quotations unarranged since to order them by any arbitrary
classification would be disloyal to their source.

> . . . the thought whereof
> Doth, like a poisonous mineral, gnaw my inwards.
>   (*Othello*, II, i, 305.)

> My affection hath an unknown bottom, like the
>   bay of Portugal.
>   (*As You Like It*, IV, i, 212.)

> When we should submit ourselves to an unknown
>   fear.
>   (*All's Well*, II, iii, 6.)

. . . it shall be called Bottom's Dream, for it hath
no bottom.
> (*A Midsummer Night's Dream,* IV, i, 221.)

. . . jugglers that deceive the eye,
Dark-working sorcerers that change the mind.
> (*The Comedy of Errors,* I, ii, 98.)

My mind is troubled, like a fountain stirr'd;
And I myself see not the bottom of it.
> (*Troilus and Cressida,* III, iii, 311.)

Macbeth: Canst thou not minister to a mind diseased;
Pluck from the memory of a rooted sorrow;
Raze out the written troubles of the brain;
And with some sweet oblivious antidote
Cleanse the stuff'd bosom of that perilous stuff
Which weighs upon the heart?
Doctor: Therein the patient
Must minister to himself.
> (*Macbeth,* V, iii, 44.)

Sleep that knits up the ravell'd sleave of care,
The death of each day's life, sore labour's bath,
Balm of hurt minds, great nature's second course,
Chief nourisher in life's feast.
> (*Macbeth,* II, ii, 35.)

Suspicion always haunts the guilty mind;
The thief doth fear each bush an officer.
> (*King Henry VI, Part III,* V, vi, 11.)

Prince: I never thought to hear you speak again.
King: Thy wish was father, Harry, to that thought.
> (*King Henry IV, Part II,* IV, v, 92.)

. . . I never may believe
These antique fables nor these fairy toys.

Lovers and madmen have such seething brains,
Such shaping fantasies, that apprehend
More than cool reason ever comprehends.
The lunatic, the lover, and the poet
Are of imagination all compact:
One sees more devils than vast hell can hold,
That is, the madman: the lover, all as frantic,
Sees Helen's beauty in a brow of Egypt:
The poet's eye, in a fine frenzy rolling,
Doth glance from heaven to earth, from earth to
    heaven;
And, as imagination bodies forth
The forms of things unknown, the poet's pen
Turns them to shapes, and gives to airy nothing
A local habitation and a name.
Such tricks hath strong imagination,
That, if it would but apprehend some joy,
It comprehends some bringer of that joy;
Or in the night, imagining some fear,
How easy is a bush supposed a bear!
       (*A Midsummer Night's Dream*, V, i, 2.)

In sooth, I know not why I am so sad:
It wearies me; you say it wearies you;
But how I caught it, found it, or came by it,
What stuff 'tis made of, whereof it is born,
I am to learn;
And such a want-wit sadness makes of me,
That I have much ado to know myself.
       (*The Merchant of Venice*, I, i,1.)

Descartes (1596–1650), by his definition of mind as awareness, may be said to have provoked, as reaction, the European
discovery of the unconscious mind. I shall therefore mark this
decisive moment by a change of technique. Descartes, as a
thinker, had no clear conception of the unconscious mind,

for to him all that is unconscious is physiological, and his physiology (like ours) could not explain how the brain works. But Descartes, the person, had at one time a very lively, efficient, and far-sighted unconscious mind which inhibited confusing emotions and gave birth to the *dream of rationalism* (that would occupy the West for centuries) *in a triple dream in course of sleep* (that occupied Descartes during a brief conversion from chaos to clarity on the night of November 10, 1619).

It is not necessary to guess what ideas actually came to Descartes for the first time during that dream sequence. What is significant is that the dreams came within a day or two of his first conceiving his plan of a unified mathematical science, and that Descartes himself believed and stated that this triple dream had determined the entire subsequent course of his life and thought. From the violent personal experience of that dream and of those few days Descartes extracted in the course of a lifetime the objective universal truth—or so he believed.

As a thinker Descartes considered that the dreams expressed a movement of the organs of the sleeper, that they constituted a language translating a desire. But to Descartes as a person the dreams were, as he said, a divine command to devote his inner life to the search for truth.

Freud considered that they were mainly dreams "from above" that could have been formed in awareness, and came only in small part from the deeper layers of the mind; that for this reason Descartes' own interpretation might be accepted, as far as it goes; and that the dreams show that Descartes was passing through a crisis of conscience associated with sexuality (perhaps his friendship with Beekman).

To these interpretations I would only add this: the dreams express the transformation of intolerable emotional conflict and confusion into a supreme (apparent) clarity in intel-

lectual awareness, achieved by a radical inhibition of all potentially confusing emotions and problems. The new start in
Descartes' life and in philosophy was made by separating conscious intellectual clarity from complex emotions which were
driven, as far as possible, into the unconscious, and from complex problems which were neglected or postponed. This
dream of rationalism betrayed human nature, but it shaped
the temperament of rationalists from Descartes to Freud.
The dreams of November 10, 1619, represented a conversion
in an extraordinarily intense personality, and hence also in
Western human nature. It is not too much to say that a new
man was born in Descartes, a new type of man in Europe, and
a new tradition in philosophy. But the new Descartes was not
whole-natured, and the new philosophy was superficial. Both
were born of impatience with painful complexity; neither
were what they claimed.

Descartes had been struggling for some time (1614–1619)
to clear his mind of prejudice and to make the pursuit of
truth his life occupation. But this aim must have provoked
deep emotional conflicts, for by the evening of November 10
he had reached the point where this endeavor (as he informs
us, writing in the third person): "threw his mind into violent
agitations that grew greater and greater. [The endeavor] so
exhausted him that the fire went to his brain and he fell into
a kind of enthusiasm which so mastered his already cast down
mind that it prepared it to receive the impressions of dreams
and visions. He [Descartes] tells us that on the 10th November, 1619, having gone to bed *wholly filled with this enthusiasm* and wholly occupied with the thought *that he had
discovered that day the foundations of the admirable science*
he had three consecutive dreams in a single night, that he
could only imagine had come to him from above." (Descartes'
italics.)

The first two dreams, recounted at great length, were

frightening: malign winds blowing Descartes from a college to a church, but not affecting other people he encounters; then a thunderstorm. Descartes explained these two dreams as representing his shortcomings and sins. The third dream had nothing frightening about it. Two books which are presented to Descartes play a central role: one a "Dictionnaire," the other a book of poetry, *Corpus Poetarum* (which existed in reality, published 1603), and in particular a poem, "Est & Non." While still asleep, so Descartes recounts, he asked himself whether he was dreaming or had had a vision. He not only decided that he was dreaming, but began, while still dreaming, to interpret the earlier part of the dream. The "Dictionnaire," he decided, stood for all the sciences, while the book of poetry stood for philosophy and wisdom.

"For he did not think that one should be so greatly astonished to see that the Poets . . . were full of sentences more serious, more felt, and better expressed than those which are found in the writings of Philosophers. He attributed this marvel to the divine nature of Enthusiasm and to the power of the Imagination, which brings out the seeds of wisdom (that are to be found in the minds of all men, like sparks of fire among the pebbles) as Reason cannot in the Philosophers."

Still asleep, Descartes continued interpreting his dream. "Est & Non" he interpreted as truth and falsehood in human knowledge and science, and he boldly persuaded himself that "it was the Spirit of Truth which had wanted to open to him the treasures of all the sciences by this dream." This last dream, Descartes says, marked out the path for the rest of his life.

After a few days Descartes regained his normal composure and began to write.

Descartes tells us that the triple dream was associated with the supreme question, "What way of life shall I follow?" and

that the dream brought him the answer as a compelling command from Heaven or Olympus: Search for the truth, by
applying the mathematical method (analytical geometry, in
the main) to all other studies. This twin experience, the
dream and the discovery of his method, did in fact put an
end to his emotional and intellectual confusions and gave a
decisive direction to his subsequent life. Olympus had spoken
through his unconscious, and Descartes had been lifted out
of his past self to acquire a new vision of truth. But his life
story proves that there remained an intense nervousness, a
disquieting sense of insecurity, producing often an impression
of insincerity, as we may easily understand. Descartes' conscious clarity was partial, and rested on a treacherous dissociation. One may suspect that all static concepts, just as they
neglect process, may produce in those who surrender their
minds to them an uncomfortable lesion. Certainly Descartes'
dogmatism regarding a split in the nature of things provoked
other thinkers, who lacked his personal dissociation, to re-
pudiate his way of thinking. Descartes' dream deserves a place
in this chapter because its consequences drew the attention
of others to the partial character of ideas so clearly expressed.

There are times when great minds seem to spring into
existence to seize great opportunities. No sooner had Descartes chosen·his path than another mind, of comparable
mathematical genius, refused to accept intellectual clarity as
ultimate, since this would mean denying prior validity to the
deepest truth he knew: the complexity of the human heart.

Pascal (1623–1662), mathematician, mystic and sage, combined a deep religious need with great introspective honesty.
He was a highly original mathematician and experienced the
attraction of mathematical clarity, but the richness and complexity of his own nature did not allow him to accept reason
as ultimate. Pascal felt that there could be no short cut to
truth. He knew Descartes personally, but rejected his phi-

losophy, and came to renounce mathematics in favor of devotion to the religious life. His revolt from nonhuman abstractions and recognition of the miserable aspects of the individual life have echoes three centuries later.

Though some texts of Pascal's *Pensées* are unreliable, and his terms, being penetrating, are difficult to translate, there can be no doubt of his insight into much that lies behind conscious reason. He uses the term "heart" (*coeur*) for his sense of the inner depths of human nature, the seat of true knowledge and of will.

The heart has its reasons, which reason knows not.

For we must not mistake ourselves, we have as much that is automatic in us as intellectual, and hence it comes that the instrument by which persuasion is brought about is not demonstration alone. How few things are demonstrated! Proofs can only convince the mind; custom makes our strongest proofs and those which hold most firmly, it sways the automaton, which draws the unthinking mind after it (*qui entraîne l'esprit sans qu'il pense*).

Those who are accustomed to judge by the heart do not understand the process of reasoning, for they wish to understand at a glance, and are not accustomed to seek for principles. And others, on the contrary, who are accustomed to reason by principles, do not at all understand the things of the heart, seeking principles and not being able to see at a glance.

It is as useless and absurd for reason to demand from the heart proofs of first principles before it will admit them, as it would be for the heart to ask from reason a feeling of all the propositions demonstrated before accepting them.

This inability should serve then only to make reason more humble, which would fain judge of all things, but not to shake our certainty, as if only reason were able to instruct us. Would to God, on the contrary, that we never needed reason, and that we knew everything by instinct and feeling! But nature has denied us this advantage, and has on the contrary given us but little knowledge of this kind, all the rest can be acquired by reason only.

. . . never does reason override the imagination, whereas the imagination often unseats reason.

Self is hateful.

May it not be better for man's happiness that he should not know himself?

B. Spinoza (1632–1677) had a vivid sense of the person as part of nature and laid stress on unconscious memory and motives as making up an unconscious personality, and hence also on the need for an objective self-knowledge reaching beneath resentment and conflict:

Men regard themselves as free, since they are aware of their will and their desires, and do not even in dream think of the causes which determine their desiring and willing, as they do not know them.

We now turn to Britain, to a remarkable group of thinkers, mainly of the English Platonist school: Sir Thomas Browne, Henry More, Ralph Cudworth, John Norris, Shaftesbury, and with them John Milton, John Dryden, and Isaac Newton.

Sir Thomas Browne (1605–1682), physician, philosopher, and theologian, sets the background with his neoclassical conception of the Idea, or *plastic life*, pervading everything, physical, organic, and mental.

Henry More (1614–1687) wrote:

The Spirit of Nature therefore . . . is a substance incorporeal, but without Sense or Animadversion, pervading the whole Matter of the Universe, and exercising a Plastical Power.

John Milton (1608–1674) in *Paradise Lost* (1667) echoes Shakespeare's view of the imagination, calling it Fancy, and distinguishing it from "mimic Fancy":

(Adam is consoling Eve for a dream she has had in which Satan tempted her)

> But know that in the soul
> Are many lesser faculties, that serve
> Reason as chief. Among these Fancy next
> Her office holds; of all external things,
> Which the fine watchful senses represent,
> She forms imaginations, aery shapes,
> Which Reason, joining or disjoining, frames
> All what we affirm or what deny, and call
> Our knowledge or opinion; then retires
> Into her private cell when Nature rests.
> Oft, in her absence, mimic Fancy wakes
> To imitate her; but, misjoining shapes.
> Wild work produces oft, and most in dreams,
> Ill matching words and deeds long past or late.
> Some such resemblances, methinks, I find
> Of our last evening's talk in this thy dream.
> But with addition strange. Yet be not sad:
> Evil into the mind of God or Man
> May come and go, so unapproved, and leave
> No spot or blame behind; which gives me hope
> That what in sleep thou didst abhor to dream
> Waking thou never wilt consent to do.

The same awareness is shown by *John Dryden* (1631–1700):

Long before it was a Play; when it only was a confused mass of thoughts, trembling over one another in the dark; when the fancy was yet in its first work, moving the sleeping images of things towards the light, these to be distinguished, and then either chosen or rejected by the judgment.

And at the same period *Isaac Newton* (1642–1727), not wishing to be troubled to give a mathematical proof of an assertion, thought it sufficient to say:

It is plain to me by the fountain I draw it from.

I have no doubt that Newton's fountain was to him divine. His genius is shown in his restriction of his science to the mathematics of an unchanging or stationary universe; the realm of creation, formation, and history was for him another matter: the direct expression of divine powers.

There are few sharp lines in the history of thought, but for convenience we shall now draw one.

Around 1680 the influence of Descartes and of the new sciences became so evident that they could not be neglected. The writers cited before Spinoza employed a primarily mystical or poetic approach, and in addition may be said either to have neglected the developing scientific attitude, or, like Pascal, to have rejected it when meditating on primary matters. We now come to a thinker who, though he shared in the classical and religious tradition and sought to maintain it, went out of his way to study science, to read the Greek atomists, and sought to disprove current scientific materialism by beating the atheistic scientists at their own game: the representation of detailed facts. It is not suggested that he was the earliest writer to attempt this after Descartes, but he is one of the most striking.

This is *Ralph Cudworth* (1617–1688), Cambridge divine, philosopher, and student of science, whose conception of a plastic power pervading nature and providing the basis for conscious thought brought him to a conception of the unconscious mind similar in many respects to our own (as has been recognized in the article on him in the *Dictionary of National Biography*). Here is Cudworth writing in 1678:

However, that there may be some vital energy without clear consciousness and express attention and animadversion, or self-perception, seems reasonable upon several accounts. For, first, those philosophers themselves, who made the essence of the soul to consist in cogitation, and again, the essence of cogitation in clear and express consciousness, cannot render it in any way probable, that the souls of men in all profound sleeps, lethargies, and apoplexies, as also of embryos in the womb, from their very first arrival thither, are never so much as one moment without expressly conscious cogitations; which, if they were, according to the principles of their philosophy, they must, *ipso facto*, cease to have any being. . . . It is certain, that our human souls themselves are not always conscious of whatever they have in them; for even the sleeping geometrician hath, at that time, all his geometrical theorems some way in him; as also the sleeping musician, all his musical skills and songs; and, therefore, why may it not be possible for the soul to have likewise some actual energy in it, which it is not expressly conscious of? We have all experience of our doing many animal actions non-attendingly, which we reflect upon afterwards; as, also, that we often continue a long series of bodily motions, by a mere virtual intention of our minds, and as it were by half a cogitation. That vital sympathy, by which our soul is united and tied fast, as it were with a knot, to the body, is a thing that we have no direct consciousness of, but only in its effects. . . . There is also a more interior kind of plastic power in the soul (if we may so call it), whereby it is formative of its own cogitations, which itself is not always conscious of; as when, in sleep or dreams, it frames interlocutory discourses betwixt itself and other persons, in a long series, with coherent sense and apt connections, in which oftentimes it seems to be surprised with unexpected wiseness and repartees, though itself were all the while the poet and inventor of the whole fable.

Elsewhere Cudworth speaks of "a drowsy unawakened cogitation," and his outlook is based on a "plastic nature," vitalized by "plastic energy."

This is the idealistic monist approach, which finds no difficulty in identifying a background to the passing moments of awareness. The book in which this quotation occurs was called *The Intellectual System of the Universe,* and its main aim was to attack Democritean materialism in the interests of the Christian religion. That controversy is not our concern here. But it is instructive that so ancient a tradition as Christian Platonism, invigorated by Cudworth's interest in contemporary physics and biology, could lead him toward ideas that we, paralyzed in our dualism, have still not got straight. If experimental physiology had been ready in 1678, or 1778, or even 1878, to support Cudworth's outlook with a scientific identification of the plastic processes of objective nature, in particular of the coordinating and formative principles in organisms and brains, the history of science and of man would have been different. If the Christian churches had seen that their best policy was to reveal the divine marvels of the human brain by encouraging physiological research, a Christian post-Cudworth school of scientific thought might have enjoyed the world prestige of Marx and Freud together, and more. But they preferred the *status quo.*

Cudworth was not alone. When John Locke, following Descartes, wrote in 1690 that "It is impossible to perceive without perceiving that he does perceive,"

John Norris (1632–1704), another English Platonist, could not let this pass and published a correction in the same year:

We may have ideas of which we are not conscious.

There are infinitely more ideas impressed on our minds than we can possibly attend to or perceive.

There may be an impression of ideas without any actual perception of them.

This was written twenty years before Leibniz expressed the same conclusions.

Norris was a disciple of *Malebranche* (1638–1715), one of the most influential French philosophers to contribute to this story, whose priority in this respect over Leibniz, with whom he corresponded, merits recognition. The following passages are from his *De la Recherche de la Vérité,* 1675.

We only know [the soul] by our consciousness, and that is why the knowledge which we have of it is imperfect; we only know of the soul what we feel taking place in us. . . . Therefore it does not suffice to know the soul completely to know what we know by our interior feeling, since the awareness we have of ourselves does not perhaps reveal to us more than the smaller part of our being.

We believe . . . that there is in the mind a capacity to receive in succession an infinity of diverse modifications which the mind itself does not know.

Shaftesbury (A. A. Cooper, Third Earl of Shaftesbury, 1671–1713) was one of the earliest English writers to give vivid expression to the sense of a dark mystery hidden in the sources of the mind, which a century later became one of the characteristic features of German romantic thought.

Know but this self. . . . O Cimmerian darkness . . . not to see which sees, which judges, which pronounces, and which only *is!* . . . Self-simple or a system? . . . What am I? A particular mind, an acting principle? . . . Or how are you yourself? . . . by a principle uniting certain parts, and that thinks and acts for these parts. . . . For my own share, I have a mind, which serves, such as it is, to keep my body and the affections of it, my appetites, imaginations, fancies, and the rest in tolerable order. . . . And the particular mind, what? . . . Part of a general mind.

Idea! Wait a while till I have examined thee, whence thou art, and to whom thou returnest.

One would think, there was nothing easier for us, than to know our own minds. . . . But our thoughts have generally such an obscure implicit language, that it is the hardest thing in the world to make them speak out distinctly.

Shaftesbury was deeply moved by this mystery, the inability of the mind to see its own sources, and he gave eloquent expression to a possible clue: the interpretation of the divine spirit of the world as a plastic force, or as he called it a *forming power* pervading everything: matter, life, and mind. The real mystery lies perhaps in the fact that Plato and his followers could guess so much, and exact science achieve so much while still failing to identify this shaping agency.

Writing at the same time, the English clergyman *George Keith* (1639–1716), after renouncing the emotional excesses of Quakerism, displayed insight into the unconscious psychology of "true" and "false" religion.

. . . the Spirit of every Heresie is no other than an exalted Imagination, joined with a perversion of Will.

[It is a necessary Christian Duty] clearly to distinguish between God's inward gracious operations and Inspirations, and all counterfeit resemblances of them.

And for the ecstasies that some of the Profets were sometimes in, it was not their own proper act, but the effect of a Divine Power and operation in them, that is far differing from what Men may seek wilfully to cast themselves into, as some have done to their great hurt.

And this is a plain demonstration of what the Quakers by a great mistake and deception call the *Life* and call it the *Life of God*

. . . when in very deed it is nothing other but the vigor and vivacity of the Animal Life and Spirits.

Also that there are Antipathies among Animals, as well as Sympathies, arising not from occult qualities, but from certain corporeal Causes, to wit, certain effluvia from one Body to another, which if agreeable, cause Sympathy, and if disagreeable, cause Antipathy; the which agreeableness or disagreeableness of those effluvia proceed not from occult qualities which the learned have generally exploded if physically understood, but from their different Texture, Figures, Motion, and Configurations.

Leibniz (1646–1716) has often been regarded as the first European thinker to give clear expression to the idea of unconscious mental activity. This may be valid if attention is restricted to writers within the scientific tradition of mathematical and logical precision—though here Pascal must not be forgotten—and it was Leibniz's careful and quasi-quantitative approach to the problem that made his conclusions so influential. He held that ordinary perceptions are the summation of countless smaller perceptions each of which we cannot be aware of, since they lie below a quantitative threshold. Leibniz also considered that these small perceptions, of which we are not directly aware, make up a wider field than those of which we are conscious.

Our clear concepts are like islands which arise above the ocean of obscure ones.

[Yet] it is not easy to conceive that a thing can think and not be conscious that it thinks.

The importance and influence of Leibniz's work is beyond question. But Malebranche and Norris had already stressed the existence of an immense background of unconscious perceptions in terms even clearer than those of Leibniz, whose originality lay mainly in the speculative idea of a quantitative threshold. This gave prestige to Leibniz's doctrine, though this threshold has never been measured. But prestige for the wrong reasons has often been a powerful influence in the history of ideas.

Stahl (1660–1734), the German chemist and physician, who gave the name "animism" to his doctrine of a world soul, held that the passions have a great influence on the state of the body, and that

disease [is] a disturbance of the vital functions caused by misdirected activities of the soul.

Vico (1668–1744), Italian lawyer, philosopher, and historian, interpreted all human thought and action as the expression of underlying laws. He is possibly the earliest writer who sought to identify a law of historical process underlying everything, including the human imagination. Though he believed that an eternal law of recurrence was displayed in the rise, maturity, and decline of all civilizations, his thinking was genetic or developmental in character and his speculative description of the earliest emergence of human society from a wild quasi-animal origin illustrates the operation of natural and divine laws in prehuman behavior, before man became humanly aware. Many passages in his works are in effect the description of unconscious mentality, of "human" judgments and actions undertaken before man became as we know him in civilized societies. The following passages are taken from his *New Science* (1725).

Our new Science must therefore be a demonstration, so to speak, of the historical fact of providence, for it must be a history of the forms of order which, without human discernment or intent, and often against the designs of men, providence has given to this great city of the human race.

. . . men were for a long time incapable of truth and reason.

. . . its start when the first men began to think humanly.

This world of nations has certainly been made by man, and its guise must therefore be found within the modification of our own human mind.

. . . the world of civil society has certainly been made by man, and its principles are therefore to be found within the modifications of the human mind.

Vico is much concerned with the origin of myths common to a whole community, which he traces to a process of selection without reflection, the operation of a sense shared by all, called by him "common sense." This is the collective unconscious at work in the genesis of myths.

Common sense is judgment without reflection.

An alternative translation of this passage is:

This meaning which is common to all is a judgment without any reflection.

He is also interested in the origin of languages, and in the peculiar status of nouns, suggesting the idea taken up two centuries later by Bergson and others, that:

nouns awaken ideas which leave firm traces.

At the same time *C. v. Wolff* (1679–1752) was engaged in clarifying and extending Leibniz's conception of unconscious mental processes. He may have been the first influential German writer to give the word *Bewusstsein* its present meaning of awareness, and his analysis of unconscious factors is clearer than that of any predecessor. For example, he asserted that less conscious ideas may be the cause of more conscious ones, and he was possibly the first to state explicitly that nonconscious factors must be *inferred* from those of which we are conscious.

Let no one imagine that I would join the Cartesians in asserting that nothing can be in the mind of which it is not aware. . . . That is a prejudice, which impedes the understanding of the mind, as we can see in the case of the Cartesians.

We conclude that we only then become conscious of objects when we distinguish them from one another; when we do not notice the difference of things which are presented to us, then we are not aware of what enters our senses.

This passage, written in 1725, expresses the view of a leading school of psychology in 1960.

Insofar as something further exists in us than we are conscious of, we must bring it to light by *inferences* from that of which we are conscious, since otherwise we should have no ground to do so. [Wolff's italics.]

Similar thoughts are expressed by Wolff's contemporary, *Lord Kames* (Henry Home, 1696–1782), Scottish judge and philosopher. In his *Essays on the Principles of Morality and Natural Religion* (1751) Kames wrote:

The whole operation of vision far surpasses human knowledge.

When we attend to the operation of the external sense, the impressions made upon us by external objects are discovered to have very different effects. In some cases we feel the impression, and are conscious of it, as an impression. In others, being quite unconscious of the impression, we perceive only the external object.

This is a remarkable passage to find written in 1751. Sir Richard Blackmore, physician and poet, in his poem *Creation* (1712) had used the word "unconscious" several times, in the more general sense of "unheeding." But Kames uses the terms "conscious" and "unconscious" in two successive sentences to characterize awareness and nonawareness in relation to particular mental functions: conscious attention to the process of receiving an impression, and perception of an object without awareness of receiving an impression. This usage overlaps with the twentieth-century meaning of unconscious mental processes. It is hard to imagine that Kames or his Edinburgh printer knew in 1751 what they were doing: sending out into the English-speaking world a new verbal symbol that would eventually mark one of the greatest revolutions in human thought. This was twenty-five years before Platner began to use *bewusstlos* in relation to mental activities.

In order again to stress the incompleteness of this survey, or rather the irrelevance of the criterion of completeness to the history of ideas, I leave to others the question how far E. Swedenborg (1688–1722), Swedish scientist, philosopher, and mystic, explicitly indicated his awareness of the importance of the unconscious mind. He certainly stressed that thought depended on the combined activity of the various parts of the brain, and it is just this correlation of separated factors which the unconscious processes prepare for the attention of the conscious mind.

If we survey the period 1670–1730 we find that during this time (after Pascal and Spinoza) not less than *eight* writers in the English, German, French, and Italian languages are known to have published ideas overlapping in some degree with our contemporary conception of unconscious mental processes: (in order of birth) *Cudworth, Malebranche, Leibniz, Norris, Vico, Shaftesbury, Wolff, and Kames.* Of these four were British, two German, one French, and one Italian. Effort has been made to eliminate national bias, but further research would probably bring to light more names in other countries.

The four British thinkers who hold such a privileged position in our story enjoyed certain advantages. First, they were not held back in their speculations by dogmatic doctrines such as Roman Catholicism or Cartesianism. Second, they were all Christian monists interested in the contemporary advances in science, who would naturally seek to identify unifying ideas linking consciousness with its background. Finally, their thinking was not inhibited by adherence to any particular scientific doctrine. These factors may all be summarized in saying that they were *freely speculating monists*. Indeed the same may be said of the other four: *Leibniz, Wolff, Malebranche, and Vico,* all of whom either inherited or sought for a monistic doctrine.

In relation to the history of the idea, Leibniz alone enjoyed an immediate and unmistakable influence, for only he worked within the new mathematical and scientific tradition of which Descartes was one of the creators. All eight were pure speculators; none of them put their ideas to any systematic observational tests. But Leibniz clothed his ideas in the borrowed uniform of quantitative science; hence his prestige and influence.

If we collect the various aspects of unconscious mental processes considered by these eight writers around 1700: memory, perception, ideas, sleep, dreams, the formative background of thought, insight, the threshold, the greater range of unconscious activities, the birth of myth, the need to infer unconscious factors, habitual activities—we find that a *considerable proportion of the general features of our present concept was already conceivable,* though in a speculative or tentative form. The main elements still missing were the link with instinct, will, and the emotions; the frequency of dissociation, conflict, and distortion; the connection with pathology, techniques for investigation, and the application to therapy; and the fusion of all these factors in a single quasi-scientific concept of the unconscious mind.

As is shown in Chart C, the *cognitive* aspects of the unconscious mind were conceivable by many isolated thinkers around 1700, while the *vital, emotional, and pathological* aspects remained to be discovered, though a mystic like Boehme, and possibly many others, had a vivid sense of the vital background which was later to become a matter of objective knowledge.

VI

The Discoverers:
1730–1800

A LITTLE KNOWN FIGURE, *C. A. Crusius* (1715–
1773), German philosopher and theologian, provides a bridge
from earlier thinkers who stressed the cognitive aspects to
those whose main interest was in the unconscious mind as the
seat of the passions. Crusius divided the faculties of the soul
into two classes: those of thinking and those of willing. For
him consciousness is an inner faculty of feeling, and external
perception can proceed without this inner awareness being
evoked. Only when it is, do we know that we are imagining,
thinking, or desiring. This inner function must operate if
mere thinking is to become conscious thinking, and it is
absent "in deep sleep, in rage, and in many other circumstances." It is a necessary condition for this inner feeling that
the external perception should pass "a certain level of live-
liness." There are many degrees of awareness.

Though Crusius has been dismissed as a negligible figure, he appears to have been one of the earliest eighteenth-century philosophers to look beneath the cognitive aspects of the unconscious mind and to assert the existence of a *Grundkraft*, a primary force or activity, of which we have no direct awareness or knowledge though it underlies all physical and mental phenomena. Kant took several ideas from Crusius, and acknowledged his importance. For us his interest lies in his early recognition, within the German philosophical tradition, that willing and thinking are twin functions of the soul of which we only become aware under special circumstances. This, however, was merely the intellectual counterpart of an emotional storm taking place at that very moment in another European.

What Crusius recognized in theory *J. J. Rousseau* (1712–1778) was experiencing with passionate intensity: the turmoil of will and emotion lying below, and often breaking through, the threshold of awareness. His almost continuous preoccupation with his own emotions led Rousseau to conceive of passive reverie as the only true happiness:

The sound of the waves and the agitation of the water holding my senses and driving every other agitation from my soul, plunged it into a delicious reverie . . . without any active cooperation of my soul.

Toward the end of his life Rousseau's chief endeavor was to achieve by continual introspection a full understanding of his own emotional nature. He did not succeed, any more than Freud did a century and a half later. Much that is obvious to us was hidden to him. But he has been called the first modern man as we know him: intensely preoccupied with his own "psychology," and lacking any reliable guide for thinking and living. Viewed biologically or historically this is the degeneracy of individualism, the loss of natural relations with family, profession, or community, in a pathological obsession with one's own frustrated emotions.

But since the West had apparently to pursue this morbid path, Rousseau must be recognized as the first to go to the limit, that is, as far as his capacities could take him. In an important sense he is the visible source of the movement which led to the discovery of the role of will and emotion in the processes that lie below the threshold. If Rousseau had not existed the movement would surely have developed, but it might have taken a different path.

Here is Rousseau reflecting on his own actions and emotions in the course of a persistent self-analysis:

It is thus certain that neither my judgment nor my will dictated my answer, and that it was the automatic consequence of my embarrassment.

There is no automatic movement of ours of which we cannot find the cause in our hearts, if we know well how to look for it there.

The true and primary motives of the greater part of my actions are not so clear to me as I have for a long time imagined.

These experiences have procured for me, by reflection, new light on my self-knowledge, and on the true motives of my conduct in a thousand circumstances on which I have so often deceived myself.

The feeling of existence alone does not imply awareness.

He did not even feel his own existence.

Beside Rousseau there appears almost at the same time a strange and influential figure, *J. G. Hamann* (1730–1788), a German philosopher of religion, who was too honest and whole-natured to accept any abstract system of thought. His power lay in his personality rather than his writings, and both Herder and Goethe derived much from him. Hamann's interest in his own experience of religious conversion, in the unconscious working of the imagination, and in contemporary biological researches, led him to recognize the temporal character of all immediate experience, and its contrast to the static abstractions of contemporary mathematical science. For him, as for Rousseau, the immediacy of experience was primary, but Hamann rejected the notion of personal isolation, and put the stress on personal relations as the basis of the individual life.

Hamann enters our story, not only because, like the *philosophes* in Paris (Diderot, Buffon, Holbach, Maupertuis, etc.), he stressed process, growth, and transformation, but also for his rejection of the autonomy of the individual consciousness, which he felt to be an instrument of superpersonal forces. Reason must patiently learn to make itself the instrument of nature, that is, of God.

But our skeleton remains hidden from us, because we were formed in secret, as though under the earth.

How much more the formation of our own ideas remains secret!

Poetry is the mother language of the human race.

Our reason must wait and hope—seek to be the servant and not the master of nature.

To be a servant of nature and to wait for the fulfillment of other births than our own.

Only patience and time are necessary.

The divine secrets of time and its development constitute nature as it is [*die reine Natur*].

Goethe valued Hamann highly, comparing him with Vico, and saying, "The main principle to which all Hamann's statements may be referred is the following: All that a man undertakes to perform, whether by deed or word or otherwise, must proceed from all his powers united: everything isolated is worthless." To which I imagine Hamann would have replied: "Yes, and to achieve this union of powers let mind be the patient servant of nature."

In England the poet *Edward Young* (1683–1765) outlined in his *Conjectures on Original Composition* (1758) a theory of the literary imagination which was deeply to influence the German romantic writers through its stress on the twin mysteries of poetic creation and of plant growth, as though some common secret underlay both.

Nor are we only ignorant of the dimensions of the human mind in general, but even of our own. . . . Therefore dive deep into thy bosom; learn the depth, extent, bias and full fort of thy mind; contrast full intimacy with the stranger within thee; excite and cherish every spark of intellectual light and heat.

An *Original* grows, it is not made.

We must now turn to see what minds of a very different kind were thinking during the same period.

David Hartley (1705–1757), philosopher and psychologist, who held that sensations are the result of vibrations of the particles in the central tissue of the nerves, wrote in 1748:

The white medullary substance of the Brain is also the immediate Instrument by which Ideas are presented to the Mind; or, in other words, whatever Changes are made in this Substance, corresponding Changes are made in our Ideas; and vice versa.

But how he did not know, nor do we. Hartley [12] in the same year defined the new science of "Psychology" as "the theory of the human Mind, with that of the intellectual principles of animals." Long before his day, in sixteenth-century Germany, the term *"Psychologia"* had begun to be used, and in 1693 the science of *"Anthropologia"* had been divided into *"Somatologia"* or anatomy, and *"Psycology."* So, in name at least, the science is nearly three hundred years old. And the "psychosomatic," or dual, approach is nearly as old, for in 1716 Davies had written of the "Psycandrick as well as Somandrick Secret."

Meantime, the main contribution of Malebranche, Norris, Leibniz, and Wolff was not forgotten, for we find *J. H. Lambert* (1728–1777), a German mathematician and physicist, noting that "in every perception there are always unnoticed parts," while *E. B. de Condillac* (1714–1780) in his *Essai sur l'Origine des Connaissances Humaines* (1746) gives a lucid analysis of the opposing views currently held with regard to unconscious perception.

Another fascinating figure is *A. Tucker* (1705–1774), English philosopher and humanist, who was intrigued by the work of the unconscious mind in tidying up what deliberate effort had left in disorder, and by the tricks of unconscious dishonesty.

. . . our [mental] organs do not stand idle the moment we cease to employ them, but continue the motions we put into them after they have gone out of our sight, thereby working themselves to a glibness and smoothness and falling into a more regular and orderly posture than we could have placed them with all our skill and industry.

Some there are who will not allow the mind to act upon motives at all, or at least assign her a limited power, which she exercises sometimes, of acting against or without them or of giving them a weight which does not naturally belong to them: they say she plays tricks with her balance, like a juggling shopkeeper who slides his little finger slily along one side of the beam, and by pressing upon it makes twelve ounces of plumbs draw up a pound of lead. It must be owned to our shame that we too frequently practice these scurvy tricks to cheat those who have dealing with us, and what is more fatal, to cheat ourselves into error and mischief; but I hope to make it appear in due time that this is done, not by a freewill of indifference overpowering the force of our motives, but by privately slipping in or stealing out the weights in either scale, which we often get a habit of doing so covertly that we are not aware of the fraud ourselves.

D. Hume (1711–1776), in his *Enquiry concerning Human Understanding* (1776) argued that all human behavior is ultimately due to instinctive or physical agencies acting in us without our knowledge:

. . . the experimental reasoning itself, which we possess in common with beasts, and on which the whole conduct of life depends, is nothing but a species of instinct or mechanical power, that acts in us unknown to ourselves; and in its chief operations, is not directed by any such relations or comparisons of ideas, as are the proper objects of our intellectual faculties.

G. C. Lichtenberg (1742–1799), German mathematician and physicist, was deeply occupied with the significance of his own dreams. He is one of the earliest examples of a professional physicist interested in the unconscious aspects of his own mental processes:

It thinks, one ought to say.

I believe that instinct takes priority over settled judgment.

One must marvel at the manifest stages of learning involved in our organization, from the most obscure contrivances to the clearest insights of reason.

We become aware of certain representations, which do not depend on us; others depend on us, or at least so we believe; where is the boundary? One should say, it thinks, just as one says, it rains. To say *cogito* is already too much, as soon as one translates it by "I think." To assume, or postulate the "I" is a practical requirement.

Unplanned wandering around, unplanned strokes of feeling, often catch the wild animal which carefully planned philosophy can use in its careful husbandry.

Lichtenberg was fascinated by his own dreams, and he had the idea, which recurs in Moritz, Schubert, Carus, Schopenhauer, and Jung, that dreams may be reminiscences of states prior to the development of individual awareness. But he was mainly concerned with the contribution which particular dreams could make to one's understanding of oneself:

I know from experience that dreams lead to self-knowledge.

I recommend dreams again. We live and feel just as much in dreams, as in waking, and the one is as much a part of our existence as the other. . . . One has hardly yet made the right use of [our knowledge of dreams].

The fact that we see ourselves in dreams is the result of the fact that we see ourselves often in a mirror, without thinking that it is in a mirror. But in dreams the image is livelier and the consciousness and thought less.

These dreams developed all kinds of ideas that were sleeping in my soul.

Dreams can serve to represent the spontaneous expression of our entire nature, without the strain of the most elaborate consideration.

Though he did not know it, Lichtenberg was not alone at that time in his concern with dreams. In 1791 *D. Simpson,* an English clergyman, published his *Discourse on Dreams and Night Visions* in which he wrote:

Dreams of great consequence in the government of the world. Of equal authority with the Bible.

And has not the experience that many men have of significant dreams and night visions a more powerful effect on their minds than the most pure and refined concepts?

We now come to an important sequence of German thinkers, from Kant, who was still mainly concerned with the cognitive aspects, to Platner, Herder, Moritz, Fichte (J. G.), Novalis, Schelling, Schlegel, and Goethe, who show a steadily deepening sense of the emotional and volitional. The sources of this new emphasis lie, if anywhere, in Shakespeare, Rousseau, and Hamann. But whatever had gone before them, in some sense the time was ripe for an outburst of emotions from the unconscious forcing men to realize that the source of feeling and willing lay in unconscious regions of the mind.

I. Kant (1724–1804) enters our story because of his great influence, rather than for any special originality.

Only we can be indirectly aware that we have a perception, though at the same time we are not directly aware of it. Such perceptions are called *dark;* the others clear.

The field of our sense perceptions and sensations, of which we are not conscious, though we undoubtedly can infer that we possess them, that is, the dark ideas in Man [and so also in animals], is immeasurable. The clear ones in contrast cover infinitely few points which lie open to consciousness; that in fact on the great map of our spirit only a few points are illuminated: this can lead us to marvel regarding our own nature.

Kant suggested that the creative activities of genius are guided by an "unconscious purpose."

E. Platner (1744–1818), physician and philosopher, is a figure of great importance. For he was apparently the first to use the German terms *bewusstlos* (unconscious) and *Unbewusstsein* (unconsciousness), and to assert that *conscious and unconscious states follow one another in a ceaseless alternation*. His *Philosophische Aphorismen* (1776) is a landmark in the history of our theme.

Consciousness is no essential part of an idea.

The soul is not always conscious of its ideas. Experience teaches this. So not always of their consequences. Thus ideas without consciousness must be possible.

Ideas with consciousness I provisionally call apperceptions, following Leibnitz; ideas without consciousness perceptions, or dark images.

The life of the mind is an unbroken series of actions, a continuous series of ideas of both kinds. For apperceptions alternate with perceptions throughout life—wakefulness and sleep, consciousness and unconsciousness.

Ideas with consciousness are often the psychological results of ideas without consciousness.

In *J. G. v. Herder* (1744–1803), a student of surgery who turned to theology and philosophy, we find, fused into a single religious and emotional vision of experience as temporal process, most of the factors which led the transformation from static to process thought: a vivid inner sense of the immediacy of change (derived partly from Rousseau, Hamann, and Eastern thought), a keen interest in archeology and history (Lessing, Winckelmann), and in the sciences (Kant, the French Encyclopedists, biology). Herder was perhaps more receptive than original. Nietzsche said that Herder "possessed in the highest degree the sense for the weather, he saw and collected the flowers of the season earlier than all the rest." Thus it is not surprising that, being inspired by a desire to bring everything into his vision, he anticipated many features of subsequent thought and was one of the earliest to give vivid expression to certain aspects of the unconscious mind. Here Herder stands halfway between the mystics and the genuine science of the unconscious that is still ahead, for he viewed the unconscious mind as the source of all power within man: the fount both of evil and of good, at once noble and terrifying.

The validity of Herder's outlook is remarkable, as far as we can judge it today. As will be seen in the following extracts he hints at many important aspects of unconscious mental processes: their demonic and frightening power; their importance as the source of human nobility, of the unifying imagination, of poetry, and of dreams; their roots in childhood experience; their role in cognition; their greater accessibility in dreams, in passion, and in illness; and the opportunity they offer for therapy and the elimination of what we see as "the great demon of evil."

Also how excellent, that it is so, and that the deepest depths of our soul are hidden in the night! Our poor thinking organ would certainly not be able to seize every stimulus, the seed of every sensation, in its ultimate elements, or to hear aloud such a soaring ocean of dark waves, without shuddering with anxiety and in fear and cowardice letting the rudder go from its hands. So mother nature took away from it whatever could not be faced by its clear consciousness, weighed every impression that it might receive, and carefully organized every channel leading to it. Now it does not analyze the roots, but enjoys the blossoms; scents float to it from the dark bushes that it neither planned nor nourished; it stands on an abyss of infinity, and knows not that it is there; thus, through this happy ignorance, it stands firm and steady.

. . . varied as the contributions of the different senses are to thinking and feeling, in our inner man everything flows together and becomes one. We usually call the depths of this confluence the *imagination* . . .

And here too often illusions and visions, illnesses and dreams, betray in the most peculiar fashion, what is sleeping within us.

So our faculty of cognition, though it is certainly the deepest *self* in us, is not so powerful, voluntary, or free, as one believes.

. . . for long, and often throughout our life, we lean on the supports given to us in earliest childhood; we think ourselves, but only in the same forms as others thought; we understand where the finger of the methods we learnt points, . . . the rest is as if it did not exist.

The ancient Germans reached decisions in drunkenness and carried them out when sober; others will reach them soberly and carry them out when drunk. Indeed it's true that our planet moves always round these two foci of our ellipse [knowing and feeling] and is seldom equally near both. Perhaps it cannot and should not; only let it be on guard against each extreme, from which it can't return. It becomes exhausted in pure reason, and sinks down into burning passion.

Every noble human characteristic sleeps, like every good seed, in motionless germ—it is there and does not know itself. . . . How can the poor germ know, and how should it know, what stimuli, forces and vapors of life flowed into it at the moment of its genesis?

If a man could sketch the deepest, most personal roots of his abstractions and feelings, of his dreams and of the paths taken by his thoughts, what a novel that would make! As it is this comes about only in illnesses and moments of passion; and what a fright-ful sight and what sheer marvel is often disclosed!

Mankind must one day get to the point where, sure of itself, it can learn to recognize that even the frustrations of our fate are caused by no one but the great and bountiful mother of all things in accordance with her eternal laws, and that the mistakes we make, and the maliciousness of others toward us, are aberrations of the human understanding and diseases of the human heart, which await our healing care. Seen in this light, the great demon of evil disappears from nature, its realm is destroyed. And the little demons in our own and in others' hearts, must never, not even in fairy tales, become co-rulers of the universe but, exposed as mistakes and phantoms, they must be stifled and reduced to silence.

A marvellous faculty in man, this involuntary and yet self-con-sistent poetic creation of fairy tales and dreams! A realm unknown to us and yet arising from out of us, in which for years, often for our entire life, we continue to live, to dream, and to wander. And precisely there we are our most severe judges. The world of dreams gives us the most serious hints about ourselves. Thus every fairy tale has the magic, but also the moral power of the dream.

Herder reacted violently against the rationalism of many scientific thinkers of his time, feeling that their intellectual abstractions distracted attention from more important aspects of experience. Now that science no longer has to struggle for prestige, scientists need not be slow to recognize that in cer-tain respects Herder was right.

We have already considered several factors which, around 1740–1760, were preparing the ground. Certainly in each decade from 1760 onward we find minds of various kinds: religious, philosophical, scientific, and clinical, paying in-creasing attention to the unconscious.

C. P. Moritz (1757–1793) founded a journal for observational psychology (*Magazin zur Erfahrungsseelenkunde*) which ran for ten years. The first two issues, in 1783, contain articles with the following titles: "Strength of Self-Consciousness," "Waking Dream," "Strange Behaviour without Consciousness," all contributed by physicians. This journal paid considerable attention to the pathology of consciousness. One article recounts how a Göttingen professor composed Greek verses in a dream, and found them next morning without any memory of the dream or even of the act of recording it. "Does not this story prove that dim ideas, that is those whose origin and relations we do not know, often determine our actions?"

J. G. Fichte (1762–1814) opens a sequence of German philosophers: Schelling, Hegel, Schopenhauer, and Nietzsche, who developed the conception of the unconscious mind as a dynamic principle underlying conscious reason. For Fichte the light of consciousness emerges out of the dark of the unconscious. The unconscious processes of the mind had previously been considered by professional philosophers to be mainly concerned with memory and perception; now they became unmistakably the seat of instinct and will.

Fichte starts, with Kant, by stressing the role of the unconscious in perception and thought:

It is this almost always neglected activity [the synthetic activity of the mind] which constructs a unity from steady contrasts, which enters between moments which must separate from each other and preserves a unity linking both; it is this alone which makes possible life and consciousness, and above all consciousness as a continuous temporal sequence.

The apperceptive faculty of the mind is an activity which contains the ultimate basis of all consciousness, but never itself comes to consciousness.

This Fichte called "the Unconscious."

But he goes on to link this Unconscious with the natural springs of action:

The highest in me, independently of consciousness and the immediate object of consciousness, is the *impulse*. The impulse is the highest representation of the intelligence in nature.

Such thoughts were certainly in the air.

Novalis (Friederich von Hardenburg, 1772–1801), the German poet, conceived man as the harmony of conscious and unconscious.

We do not know the depth of our mind. The secret path leads inward. Inside us, or nowhere, are the realms of eternity, the past and the future.

Equation and analogy between the theory of body and of mind.

Then psychology and physiology would seem to me to be completely identical, and the mind nothing but the *principle of the system*.

The person is a harmony . . . not a mixture, nor a movement. . . . Spirit and person are one.

One is necessarily terrified when one casts a glance into the depths of the mind. The depths of meaning and the will know no limits. . . . The imagination is exhausted and ceases to operate, only its momentary constitution is perceived. Here we encounter the possibility of mental illnesses . . . and the moral law appears as the one true, great elevating principle of the universe, as the basic law of all harmonious development.

Strange that the inside of man has thus far been so scantily observed and unintelligently discussed. . . . How little one has applied physics to the human spirit, and the spirit to the external world. Reason, imagination, intelligence—these are the bare frame-work of the universe operating in us. No word of their wonderful blendings, new forms, and transitions. No one has thought of seeking out a new unknown force, to follow out their cooperative relationships. Who knows, what wonderful new unities, what wonderful new developments, still lie ahead of us within ourselves.

Between 1775 and 1800 the study of human personality by physicians was breaking fresh ground and a movement was initiated which laid the basis for the medical psychology of the nineteenth and twentieth centuries. Only a few realized this at the time.

In retrospect we can see that one of the most influential was *F. A. Mesmer* (1733–1815), who claimed to achieve permanent cures of mental illnesses by overcoming consciousness through the use of "animal magnetism." The importance of what is now called suggestion both in inducing and in curing hysterical conditions was known to the ancient Greeks. Mesmer provided a transition from the ancient mysteries to true medical research. He did not himself employ controllable methods and he gave no acceptable explanation of his partial success. But the results which he achieved by hypnotism provoked the interest of the French psychiatrists whose work gave Freud his opportunity.

Another important influence was *J. G. Cabanis* (1757–1808), a French physician who emphasized the physiological background of mind, and held that a physical understanding of man must provide the true basis for philosophy and ethics. Cabanis' philosophy may be called a physiologically differentiated animism. His studies of the effect of physiological states on the mind led him to the idea which had occurred to Descartes: in order to influence character, modify the organism. Cabanis' combination of a highly scientific approach with a firm conviction that his science held great promise for man played a considerable part in stimulating several of the leading nineteenth-century figures in our story, such as Schopenhauer, Maine de Biran, and von Hartmann, though for Cabanis physiology was all-important, and the activities of the mind were particularly influenced by those of the reproductive system.

Often the energy or weakness of the mind, the elevation of genius, the abundance and élan of its ideas, or their almost complete absence and the impotence of the intellectual organs, depend entirely and directly on the states of excessive activity, languor, or disorder in which the *organs of generation* find themselves. [My italics.]

The source of morality lies in the human organization, on which depend both our faculties and our manner of feeling.

J. C. Reil (1759-1813), a German physician, was concerned with questions which he was one of the earliest to pose clearly: "Which illnesses are psychic in origin? Which of these should be treated by psychic and which by physical methods?" Here is a sample from a work published after his death, but written around 1790:

The passions act powerfully on the organism, can make it sick, and kill it. But by the same powers they have also the capacity under certain circumstances to cure it.

For Reil the clue to the nature of man lay beneath what is directly visible of body and mind in principles of *centrality* and *tension*.

During this period interest in the interactions of body and mind was growing rapidly among physicians. Though Cabanis' view that physiology was primary was the most popular, the reverse position, that the mind influenced bodily states, was also being expressed. For example, in Germany

J. G. Langermann (1768–1832) published a work, "On a Method of Diagnosing and Curing Morbid States of Mind," (in Latin) in 1797, where he developed the view that many physical diseases were of psychological origin and stressed the need to treat them by psychotherapy.

J. G. E. Maass (1766–1823), German philosopher, was interested in the expression of desire in sleep and in dreams.

Passion is also an activity of the mental faculty, more precisely of the faculty of desire. But sleep may often be too deep for us to be conscious of the passion which disturbs it and of the associated images but not less often it happens that a dream is born. For if an idea reaches our consciousness during sleep, then a dream is present.

F. W. J. v. Schelling (1775–1854), a close friend of Goethe, and representative of the German School of *Naturphilosophie,* though often unclear and overabstract, is of considerable importance as a link in the chain of thinkers leading from the mysticism of Boehme to the protoscience of Freud.

For Schelling unconscious nature is potential mind, intelligence in course of development. Unconscious nature becomes conscious in the Ego. Consciousness is a secondary phenomenon due to the conflict of subject and object. A single unconscious formative energy underlies everything and displays a movement toward consciousness.

Aesthetic activity is an interplay of conscious and unconscious mind beyond the reach of rational analysis.

In all, even the commonest and most everyday [human] production, there cooperates with the conscious an unconscious activity.

Man's noblest activity is that which knows not itself.

The identity of conscious and unconscious in the self.

The eternal unconscious, that is also the eternal sun in the realm of the mind, conceals itself by its own undulled light, and though it never becomes an object, nonetheless impresses all spontaneous activities with its identity, and is at the same time for all intelligence the invisible root of which intelligence itself is only an expression.

You demand that you must be conscious of this freedom? But do you realize that only because of it is all your consciousness possible? Do you realize that the "I," as far as it arises in consciousness, is no more the unmixed absolute "I" . . . ? Self-consciousness implies a danger of losing the "I."

Schelling gave the earliest formulation known to me of the following argument, which for minds affected by the Cartesian dualism is of crucial importance: *that one organizing principle must pervade both the physical world and consciousness, but that outside our own awareness this principle is not itself conscious.* This unifying principle of organization and productivity operates without awareness in the determinism of nature, and with awareness in our sense of freedom. We have to use our awareness to infer this principle where we are not directly aware of it, both in the rest of nature and in the unconscious formative processes of our own minds.

It is impossible to understand how the objective world adjusts to our ideas, and simultaneously how our ideas adjust to the objective world, if a pre-established harmony does not exist between the two worlds: the ideal and the real. But this pre-established harmony is inconceivable unless the activity which produces the objective world is originally identical with the activity which expresses itself in the will, and vice versa.

The same activity, which in free actions is productive with consciousness, must in producing the world be productive without consciousness.

But this separation [of self from object] is only a means, not an end. For the nature of man is action. But the less he thinks about himself the more active he is. His noblest activity is that which is not aware of itself. Once he makes himself an object, the *whole* man no longer acts, for he has stopped a part of his activity in order to reflect about the remainder.

As without language not only no philosophy, but no human consciousness at all is conceivable, the foundations of language could not have been consciously laid; and yet the deeper we penetrate into it, the more clearly does it appear that its invention far surpasses in profundity those of the highest conscious product. It is with language as with human beings; we think we behold them come blindly into existence, and at the same time cannot doubt their unfathomable significance even in the smallest particular.

It has been suggested that Schelling's "Unconscious" lies purely in the cognitive realm, like Kant's unconscious apperceptive activity. This may be true of Schelling's temperament as a thinker, but not of the actual content of certain of his writings, as will be seen from these quotations, which stress the primary role of will and action. "For the nature of man is active." Here, with unmistakable clarity, is the primary element in all those views of man which have displaced naïve rationalism: the Romantic, the neobiological, and recent psychological theories.

J. W. v. Goethe (1749–1832) had the advantage of being primarily a poet (but one with an intense interest both in visual and in emotional experience) and he distrusted those static analytical abstractions which for him patently neglected the organized form that constitutes the characteristic feature of everything in nature and man. It is significant that for a few years after 1784 Goethe collaborated with Herder in making a study of the natural sciences, both of them believing that Kant's analytical approach to science was inadequate. With Goethe's fascination in immediate phenomena, including his own imagination and emotions, and his sensitivity to the thoughts germinating in his contemporaries, it is not surprising that, read in retrospect, he appears vividly aware, with the Romantic poets and the others already quoted, of the role of unconscious mental activities. The shift of emphasis from the cognitive toward the instinctive and vital aspects goes a step further in Goethe. Though less analytically philosophical and objectively scientific than many others before and after, his outlook is more balanced. His intuition is single, and for him as for Novalis, consciousness and unconsciousness, properly interpreted, are inseparable, mere names for complementary aspects of one phenomenon.

For Goethe, as for Spinoza whom he greatly admired, everything human is part of nature. The poetic imagination is one with the deepest secret of nature, for the primary process in everything is the coming into existence of form (*Gestaltung*). The working of his own poetic fantasy is a natural process.

His imagination is a gift, "pure nature." It operates "involuntarily, even against my will." He wrote Werther "practically unconsciously." The same theme echoes through all his writings; it is the most powerful clue to his outlook, since the imagination, for him, underlies all loving, willing, and thinking. It is this concern with the background of the human mind and imagination that led Jung to interpret the second part of *Faust* as "a preoccupation with the unconscious."

Here are a few samples of Goethe's *aperçus*, taken at random from an immense number.

Was von Menschen nicht gewusst,
Oder nicht gedacht,
Durch das Labyrinth der Brust,
Wandelt in der Nacht.

Man cannot persist long in a conscious state, he must throw himself back into the Unconscious, for his root lives there.

Men are to be viewed as the organs of their century, which operate mainly unconsciously.

Everything that we call invention or discovery, in the higher sense, is the significant practising, exercising of primitive feeling for truth, which, after a long and quiet development, leads unexpectedly and with lightning speed to a fertile recognition. It is a revelation developing from the internal toward the external, which gives man a glimpse of his likeness to God. It is a synthesis of world and spirit, which gives a blissful assurance of the eternal harmony of existence.

Goethe had a firm conviction that conscious and unconscious are inextricably interwoven in the working of the mind and that cooperation of the two aspects was essential to all the greatest achievements of the creative imagination in any realm. He gave the clearest expression to this in a letter to W. v. Humboldt, written in 1832, five days before his death at the age of eighty-three.

Every action, and so every talent, needs some inborn element which acts of itself, and unconsciously carries with it the necessary aptitudes, and which, therefore, works spontaneously in such a way that, though its law is implicit in it, its course in the end may be aimless and purposeless. The earlier man becomes aware that there exists a craft, an art that can help him toward a controlled heightening of his natural abilities, the happier he is . . .
Here begin the manifold relations between the conscious and

the unconscious. Take for instance a talented musician, compos-
ing an important score: consciousness and unconsciousness will
be like warp and weft, a simile I am fond of using. Through practice, teaching, reflection, success, failure, furtherance and resistance, and again and again reflection, man's organs unconsciously
and in a free activity link what he has acquired with his innate
gifts, so that a unity results which leaves the world amazed . . .

F. Schiller (1759–1805) poet and dramatist, and also friend
of Goethe, shows a similar awareness: "Poetry sets out from
the unconscious." He advised a friend to release his imagination from the restraint of critical reason by employing a flow
of free associations.

Although by the dim light of everyday emotions the secret working of the forces of desire remain hidden away from light, it
becomes all the more conspicuous and stupendous when passion
is strongly aroused. . . . If for the other realms of nature there
should arise a Linnaeus to classify impulses and inclinations he
would greatly astonish mankind.

It will be noted that in the eighteenth century the unconscious mind had already been linked with a primary organizing activity or formative principle, with the organs of generation and the *élan* of desire, and with illness. The nineteenth
century developed these early speculations in various directions, but added little that was new to the general conception.

VII

The Discoverers:
1800–1850

THE DEVELOPMENT of the idea of the uncon-
scious mind during the eighteenth and nineteenth centuries
followed two main paths which can be considered separately,
though a few thinkers combined both.

The first was to continue the scientific examination of detailed facts, approaching the unconscious mental processes
in the individual cautiously from the clearly known facts of
the conscious life, from above as it were. This is the path of
Leibniz, Kant, Herbart, Benecke, Wundt, Hamilton, Maudsley, Fechner, Lipps, and countless others who contributed to
the new science of psychology. This "inductive" school is
fully treated in the histories of psychology, and will therefore here be given a smaller place than is its due.

Those who took the other path sought to identify at one
stroke the general character of all unconscious processes,

either in nature as a whole or in the human mind, either individual or collective. The most important examples within philosophy are Hegel, Schelling, Schopenhauer, Nietzsche, and perhaps von Hartmann (though he claimed to hold a balance between his central idea and its particular expressions). They dived straight into the unknown, deserting step-by-step reasoning for a plunge into the depths. These four, and their followers, were in an important sense anti-Classical, anti-European, and anti-Enlightenment, for they rejected the progressive advance of knowledge by careful discrimination and instead postulated universal "dynamic" principles with which the conscious person could identify himself and his emotions, and from which everything else could be "deduced." They preferred a dynamic of feeling to the apparent clarity of analytical thought.

The disputes between the two schools were riddled with misconceptions, for both points of view were indispensable. The intellect must hold to individual facts, yet without intuitive raids into new realms the analytical, step-by-step approach would lack constructive hypotheses and a direction of advance. Enthusiastic vision and detailed precision are both necessary, though they are seldom found together, as they were, for example, in Kepler.

The Romantic raid into the dark realms of the soul is well illustrated by *J. P. F. Richter* (Jean Paul, 1763–1825), German novelist, who gave lively expression in the first years of the nineteenth century to the sense of the unconscious as the seat of the passions, emotions, and the creative spirit of man. Jean Paul had studied under Platner, from whom he had learned of the Leibniz-Wolff conception of the unconscious. But in Jean Paul the cognitive aspect falls into the background, the unconscious is now (1804) the source of vitality, the unknown "inner Africa."

The unconscious is really the largest realm in our minds, and just on account of this unconsciousness the inner Africa, whose unknown boundaries may extend far away. Why should everything come to consciousness that lies in the mind since, for example, that of which it has already been aware, the whole great realm of memory, only appears to it illuminated in small areas while the entire remaining world stays invisible in the shadows? And may there not be a second half world of our mental moon which never turns toward consciousness?

The most powerful thing in the poet, which blows the good and the evil spirit into his works, is precisely the unconscious. So a great one, like Shakespeare, will enfold and present jewels which he could no more see than he could his own heart in his body, since the divine wisdom always expresses its fullness in the sleeping plant, in the animal instinct and in the movements of the soul. . . . If one dares to say anything about the unconscious and unfathomable, then one can only seek to determine its existence, not its depths.

Visual artists and poets are among the most sensitive barometers of the intellectual weather, and it would be of interest to examine how in Germany and Britain they responded in their different ways, and at different times in their lives, to the emerging idea of the unconscious, say between 1770 and 1830, the period of Goethe's adult life. To take four poets: Goethe, Schiller, Wordsworth, and Coleridge were all aware of the new realm being explored, though in accordance with their contrasted temperaments they showed this in different ways.

W. Wordsworth (1770–1850) in "The Prelude" (1805) reveals his preoccupation with the hidden sources of his own thoughts:

I held unconscious intercourse with beauty.

Caverns there were in my mind which sun could
    never penetrate.

With meditations passionate from deep recesses
    in my heart.

Just as we are, the immortal spirit grows
Like harmony in music; there is a dark
Inscrutable workmanship that reconciles
Discordant elements.

                . . . my brain
Worked with a dim and undetermined sense
Of unknown modes of being; o'er my thoughts
There hung a darkness, call it solitude
Or blank desertion.

S. T. Coleridge (1772–1834), as poet, philosopher, and wide
reader, is as much aware of the new outlook as anyone of
his generation, but he retains a unique place for "reason,"
by which he means rational awareness in the service of the
whole man. Like Goethe and Schiller he recognizes the subtle
interplay of conscious and unconscious in artistic creation:

In every work of art there is a reconcilement of the external with
the internal; the consciousness is so impressed on the unconscious
as to appear in it.

that state of nascent existence in the twilight of imagination and
just on the vestibule of consciousness.

the twilight realms of consciousness.

The interest in dreams was carried further by *G. H. v.
Schubert* (1780–1860) who, in 1840, published a book on the
"Symbolism of Dreams." The following quotations are taken
from earlier works (1808, 1838):

And just as our body in a healthy condition knows and notices nothing of what happens inside it to the food and air which has been taken in, so also is the internal psychological process of assimilation under ordinary conditions unnoticed, unconscious, and only recognizable through its results.

Nonetheless there have been in the past and still occur states of the human being in which his spirit attains a direct knowledge of the spiritual and divine, and his mind knowledge of the internal, hidden psychological world.

Also in the life of the mind a continual rhythm of inner events can be observed which the comparing reason, without prejudicing the truth, might compare with the sleeping and waking of the body . . . for just as sleep strengthens the limbs for the tasks of the day . . . so this retreat of our mind from the active direction to the passive, which we can compare with sleep, strengthens all the powers and capacities of the human mind and prepares in them the beginnings of a new, fresh movement along the road of active operation.

Maine de Biran (1766–1824), French philosopher, is another important figure. De Biran was a self-taught introspective thinker mainly concerned with problems of perception and epistemology, but he went beyond most of the earlier systematic thinkers in giving a primary role to vitality, will, and effort. For him awareness is a consequence of some challenge to the inner, often unconscious, will.

De Biran was particularly influenced by Leibniz, Condillac, and Cabanis. There is much in common between De Biran's doctrine and that of Schopenhauer, who was writing at the same period, and he may also have been interested in Mesmer's work. De Biran studied Pascal closely and critically. Like Schopenhauer, he contrasts the conscious ego with the unconscious background which ultimately controls it, predetermining character and intelligence. Janet goes so far as to give De Biran credit for the "first clear recognition of the unconscious." I have already quoted enough to show that this is misleading, but these passages, written between 1808 and 1812, speak for themselves:

Between the full consciousness and the Cartesian mechanism there is room for beings with sensation without awareness, without a *me* capable of perceiving it.

"Affection" is defined by De Biran as "what remains of a complete sensation when one removes the personal individuality or me." This constitutes the mode "of a multitude of living beings whose condition we approach whenever our intellectual thinking is weakened or degraded, when thought falls asleep, when the will is absent, when the me is as though absorbed into the impressions, when the moral personality no longer exists."

Our illustrious Montaigne says with his directness and usual profundity: "There is not a single organ which does not often operate against our will; each organ has its own passion which awakes it and puts it to sleep without our leave."

How many facts, and direct impressions, combine to demonstrate these passions, which one might call partial, indicated with such truth and force by the author of the *Essays:* is it not thus that even during the silence of the sense and the imagination an internal organ, such as that of hunger or of the sexual appetite, spontaneously awakes all of a sudden, draws to itself all the faculties of sensibility, masters the will, absorbs the intelligence, changes the direction of the ideas, the order of all the movements and impresses a sequence of determinations and actions correctly described as animal, so much so that the *me* does not take a truly active part in it and that they equally take place without its cooperation, as in the instincts or in somnambulism . . .

These secret motive powers of a crowd of actions and of determinations remain none the less profoundly unknown to the sensible being who obeys them, and are hidden to reflection owing to their very intimacy . . .

It is such dispositions, whether variable or constant, which, unperceived by the sense, combine their products, impregnating —one may say—the objects and images with certain colorings, certain affective modifications which appear truly to belong to them and to adhere to them. Hence that refraction of the sensibility which shows us external nature now as smiling and gracious, now as covered by a funeral veil, which makes us see in the same things, the same beings, now objects of hope and love, now matters for distrust or fear; thus there is "hidden" in these obscure impressions, which we cannot reverse, the source of practically all the good and evil linked to the various moments of our life, we carry there within us the truest sources of all good and evil . . . and we accuse chance, we build altars to blind and variable fortune! In fact what does it matter whether this secret power is inside or outside us! For is not this the *fate* which pursues us, directs us, and draws us often without our knowing . . . let us have the courage to say it, and who better than you, Gentlemen [*De Biran was speaking to an audience of physicians*], have the right to appreciate this assertion which others, perhaps, will judge as too daring? It is not at all in the power of philosophers, of reason, or even of virtue, all-powerful as it is in relation to the volition and actions of the man of goodwill, by itself to create any of these happy affections which can make the immediate experience of life so sweet, nor to change those sinister dispositions which can make it so insupportable? If there existed some methods for producing such results, it would be in your art above all, it would be in physical medicine as much as moral medicine that one should look for them; and whoever discovers such a precious secret, acting on the very source of the internal sensibility, should be regarded as the first benefactor of the species, the dispenser of the supreme good, of wisdom, and even of virtue—if one can call virtuous whoever is always good without effort, being always calm and happy . . .

In order to recognize the proper and specific characteristics of those immediate impressions, whose source is in the internal life and which exercise such a far-reaching and powerful influence on all faculties of man, one must catch these characteristics when they are isolated or dominant in cases where the functions of the active life are still quiet or awaiting activity, or in a momentary state of suspension, sluggishness or transformation. . . . The phenomena of the life of the *fetus* during the period of gestation, those of sleep and delirium, and those finally of various affective sympathies can provide here interesting data and curious examples.

Hence those remarkable dreams through which a suffering nature has sometimes revealed the cause and basis of his ill, explained his needs, and indicated the appropriate remedies.

Observe, in fact, that even in the state of waking certain general laws of association direct the sequence of the spontaneous images of our mind, or determine the combinations or aggregates that these form in our head; aggregates all the more resistant to the methods of analysis, and all the more inaccessible to reflection, because they are formed of their own accord, following the arbitrary dispositions in the brain, without any intervention of the active faculties or of the power of the will.

A perception or an image that enters the mind without making any trace in the memory, can nonetheless serve to introduce other ideas which are linked to them by the laws of association.

[A consideration of dreams shows:]
1. The contrast between two principles of action which unite to constitute the nature of man with his diverse faculties: the one subordinated to the vitality of the organs and to the animal sensibility; the other which is liberated from them up to a certain point and obeys hyperorganic laws;
2. The suspension of this latter principle in the phenomena of sleep and dreams: a fact which is general and common, supported by the most varied phenomena of this class.

Maine de Biran was in regular correspondence around 1810 with A. M. Ampère (1778–1836), the physicist, and Ampère's letters to De Biran have been published. Ampère discusses the nature of sensation, the origin of the sense of "Me," and suggests that without this self-awareness sensation is an animal function lacking the characteristics of true experience, as we know it. This correspondence does not lend itself to quotation, as the two friends took for granted what they knew they shared: certain convictions about the unconscious aspects of mental activities.

The next quotation is one of my favorites.

I. P. V. Troxler (1780–1866) was a German-Swiss physician, teacher, and philosopher, who had studied under Schelling. This is taken from his *Glimpses into the Nature of Man* (1812):

Voluptuousness is a kind of wisdom of the unconscious, and beauty a kind of freedom of the involuntary, but life has married the unconscious and involuntary to the reasonable and spontaneous—and so man should not separate what heaven has joined.

G. W. F. Hegel (1770–1831), though an important figure in the history of ideas, and one of the first to attempt to systematize a universal doctrine of process, made scarcely any novel contribution to the conception of unconscious mental activities. Yet his thought is pervaded with the sense of an unconscious historical movement often becoming in man an unconscious will, as in these passages:

The patterns of habit affect all types and levels of activity of the mind; the external, spatial determination of the individual, that he stands upright, made by his will into a habit, is a direct, unconscious attitude which none the less remains a matter of his persisting will.

The History of the World begins with its general aim—the realization of the Idea of Spirit—only in an *implicit* form, that is as Nature; a hidden, most profoundly hidden, unconscious instinct; and the whole process of History is directed to rendering this unconscious impulse a conscious one.

Manifestations of vitality on the part of individuals and peoples, in which they seek and satisfy their own purposes, are, at the same time, the means and instructions of a higher and broader purpose of which they know nothing—which they realize unconsciously.

[Of Caesar] it was not, then, his private gain merely, but an unconscious impulse that occasioned the accomplishment of that for which the time was ripe. Such individuals [the World Historical Heroes] had no consciousness of the general idea they were unfolding.

A. Schopenhauer (1788–1860) made the idea of an unconscious will in nature and man the center of his thought and developed this idea with great vigor and psychological insight, chiefly in his main work: *The World as Will and Idea.* He touched on most aspects of the unconscious as we think of it today and, as we have seen, the ground had been prepared for a century and a half. I have chosen the following as an example, not of the power and breadth of his vision, but of his early understanding of a special problem: the origins of mental illness.

The exposition of the origin of madness . . . will become more comprehensible if it is remembered how unwillingly we think of things which powerfully injure our interests, wound our pride, or interfere with our wishes; how easily . . . we unconsciously break away or sneak off from them again. . . . In that resistance of the will to allowing what is contrary to it to come under the examination of our intellect lies the place at which madness can break in upon the mind . . .

If . . . certain circumstances become for the intellect completely
suppressed . . . the gaps which arise are filled up at pleasure;
thus madness appears. For the intellect has given up its nature to
please the will; the man now imagines what does not exist. Yet
the madness which has thus arisen is now the lethe of unendur-
able suffering; it was the last remedy of harassed nature, i.e. of
the will.

The psychoanalyst Otto Rank suggested that Schopenhauer
includes under madness what is now called neurosis.

In England at this time *Thomas de Quincey* (1785-1859),
"the prince of dreamers", declared in his "Palimpsest of the
Human Brain" that unconscious principles in the mind
sustain its unity during its last moments, as death is approaching, and at times of crisis:

The fleeting accidents of a man's life, and its external shows, may
indeed be irrelate and incongruous; but the organising principles
which fuse into harmony, and gather about fixed predeterminate
centres, whatever heterogeneous life may have accumulated from
without, will not permit the grandeur of the human unit greatly
to be violated, or its ultimate repose to be troubled, in the retrospect from dying moments, or from other great convulsions.

The idea that the unconscious mind might be a crucial
factor in the cure of mental or physical disorders, which—
except in mesmerism—had previously been mainly speculative, became a practical issue for a few physicians around
1820–1830.

A. J. F. Bertrand (1801–1831), a French doctor, was partly
occupied with the task of turning Mesmer's experiences into
a genuine therapeutic science. He defined "ecstasy" as "a particular state, which is neither wakefulness, nor sleeping, nor
dreaming, nor a sickness, but a state natural to man," and
discusses this in saints, prophets, miracle-workers, the pos-

sessed, and those in convulsions. Bertrand explains how unerringly "instinct" can sometimes speak through the words of a somnambulist:

But when the somnambulist says things which can be the direct result of judgments which their intelligence makes with regard to impressions they have received, one can accord the greatest confidence to wnat they say. Such notions fall into the class of instinctive notions.

So their anticipations, the sense for remedies, understanding of illnesses, etc., yield results of which one can be proud, provided always that one can assure oneself that the somnambule, in speaking, is listening only to the inspiration of his instinct.

In the same decade *J. F. Herbart* (1776–1841), German philosopher, psychologist, and educationist, made an important step forward toward a theory of the structure and mode of operation of the unconscious mind. In a general sense the unconscious mind had already been discovered, for the necessity for inferring unconscious mental activities had been well established. Moreover, in a tentative and speculative manner many thinkers in different cultures had already divided the mind into two or three higher and lower parts; the Egyptians, the Hebrews, the Hindus, and the medieval Christians, had all done this. But within Europe after 1600 few thinkers, if any, had attempted to reformulate these ancient structural doctrines and to render them fertile by introducing further principles of functional operation. Herbart's ideas, published from 1824 onward, therefore mark an important step.

As we have seen, the context of thought had been prepared for this. Not only had the general conception of unconscious mental activities become widely acceptable, and even commonplace, to an influential school of advanced poetic, philosophical, and scientific thinkers, but the idea of maturing this conception so that it could be applied to achieve deeper understanding and possibly even therapy had begun to grip enterprising minds.

Countless physicians had been saying from 1780–1820: "Don't exaggerate the importance of consciousness." The terms "psychosomatic" and "somatopsychic" had been used by German physicians in 1818 and 1822. The treatment of pathological mental conditions was already a legitimate field of specialization for those with medical training. The "dynamic" or developmental way of thinking had been maturing for over fifty years. It is indeed difficult to imagine that hypotheses regarding the precise structure of the formative and destructive processes within the psyche could have been long postponed.

Herbart's contribution was to suggest that all mental phenomena result from the actions and interactions of "ideas" (presentations); that ideas are of different kinds, stronger and weaker; that arrested (inhibited) ideas are obscured and disappear from consciousness, leaving the field to others; that such inhibited, unconscious ideas constitute a mass and continue to exert their pressure against those in consciousness; and that there is thus a continual conflict between conscious and unconscious ideas at the threshold of consciousness. This is a positive theory regarding the mode of operation of the mind, and Herbart carried it further: in his view the strong ideas may not be old ones, new ideas may be capable of defeating and inhibiting long-established conceptions. Herbart's "ideas" are evidently active agents expressing vital tendencies, and their struggles reflect the progressive adaptation of the mind to personal and social situations.

One of the older ideas can in this situation be completely driven out of consciousness by a new much weaker idea. On the other hand its pressure there is not to be regarded as without effect;

rather it works with full power against the ideas which are present in consciousness. It thus causes a particular state of consciousness, though its object is in no sense really imagined.

The importance of Herbart's ideas, and their influence on much subsequent thought, including Freud's, has been widely discussed. We are now entering the period when the history of the idea of the unconscious in clinical and theoretical psychopathology is covered by the standard histories of medical psychology.

It is clear that the prestige of Herbart's ideas, like those of Leibniz, lay in the fact that he presented them in quantitative form, as a speculative mechanics of the mind. But in 1960 this has still not been justified. Indeed, it is doubtful if it can have any objective meaning to assert that "at a particular moment in A's mind an abstract representation of a Platonic Moral Ideal had half of the strength of a concrete representation (say) of Venus." (An ordering relation may exist, but a quantitative measure is probably irrelevant.)

Herbart's ideas did not evoke any immediate response, for few thinkers of the time were ready to recognize that unconscious ideas might be, and frequently are, active agents in a conflict on the threshold.

For example, *F. E. Benecke* (1798–1854), writing in 1825, recognized a tendency to pass from unconscious to conscious states, and a principle of alternation in the mind as a whole, but the idea of conflict is missing.

[The newly born child's] sensations and apprehensions are all of them as yet *unconscious*.

These unconscious powers possess from the very first an inherent capacity of becoming conscious. . . . Consciousness, therefore, does not exist from the first in any soul; it must come into existence gradually.

. . . in the developed soul there is a perpetual alternation of consciousness and unconsciousness.

. . . *involuntary suggestions,* not to be confused with involuntary impressions, which often arise suddenly in the soul . . .

Similar ideas were also being expressed in France.

Thus *J. J. S. de Cardaillac,* in a philosophical work published in 1830, wrote:

One must note also that, amidst this immense crowd of ideas always presented to the mind, it is only a small number that are distinctly perceived and felt; and, among this small number, one must include those which, being expressed by the vocal or mental speech, are actually the object of attention; those which are most closely related to circumstances which particularly strike us of their own accord, or which acquire dominance by the attention we give to them. As for the others, even though they are neither perceived nor experienced, they are no less present to the mind, playing there a most important role, as motives determining action; and the influence they exert in this manner becomes the more important the better they are disguised by habit.

At the same time, in 1832, *C. Nodier* (1780–1844), novelist and poet, a much traveled thinker and friend of many Romantic writers, was publishing his ideas on sleep, dreams, and the depths of the mind:

It may seem extraordinary, but it is certain that sleep is not only the most powerful condition, but even the most lucid condition for thought, if not in the transitory illusions in which it envelops its thought, at least in the perceptions which derive from it.

Folk wisdom has expressed this truth in the liveliest manner in the significant usages of all languages: I'll sleep on it . . . the night will bring counsel.

Great God! Who will ever sound the impenetrable mysteries of the spirit, whose depth makes dizzy the most confident reason?

Since there are two powers in man, or if one may so express it, two spirits which rule him [the imaginative principles of sleep, and the positive materialistic principle of waking] . . . which is the better of the two states? If I dare to state my opinion, since man cannot escape, along some unknown tangent, the obligation of accepting and fulfilling the conditions of his double nature, both are impossible in an exclusive application. . . . In a country where the positive principle claims to reign over all opinions, there is nothing left to do but to renounce the name of man and to retire to the woods . . . for such a society doesn't deserve any other farewell.

While Nodier was dreaming of an escape from man's dual nature by a retreat into the woods (perhaps taking Shakespeare and Goethe with him), *S. A. Kierkegaard* (1813–1855), the Danish philosopher, was seeking to pass beyond despair by deep introspection, penetrating through the layers of unconscious distortions to reach, with Boehme, a redeeming vision of the Christian message of spiritual harmony.

Despair, viewed so that one does not consider whether it is conscious or unconscious. . . . If the Self is not true to itself, then it is in despair, whether it knows it or not.

The degree of consciousness is as it were the exponent of the power of the despair: the more consciousness the more intense the despair. . . . The minimum of despair is a state which . . . in a kind of innocence does not even know that it is despair, and this coincides with the minimum of consciousness. It can then even

seem questionable to the observer whether he is at all right to
call such a state despair.

The despair that does not know it is despair.

Sir W. Hamilton (1788–1856), student of medicine, law,
and metaphysics, was one of the earliest English-speaking
scientific philosophers to accept and develop, in lectures given
from 1836 onward, the ideas being promoted in Germany:

Are there, in ordinary, Mental modifications, i.e. Mental activities
and passivities—of which we are unconscious, but which manifest
their existence by effects of which we are conscious?

I do not hesitate to affirm that what we are conscious of is con-
structed out of what we are not conscious of. . . . The Mental
modifications in question . . . are not in themselves revealed to
consciousness; but as certain facts of consciousness necessarily suppose them to exist, and to exert an influence on the [conscious]
Mental processes, we are thus constrained to admit, as Modifications of Mind, what are not phenomena of Consciousness.

The sphere of our conscious modifications is only a small circle
in the centre of a far wider sphere of action and passion, of which
we are only conscious through its effects.

Hamilton's systematic and comprehensive approach to the
problem, and his emphasis on action and passion, contributed
to the development of an English school, whose most influential members were Carpenter, Morell, and Maudsley. This
school directly influenced Freud's teachers in Vienna.

K. F. Burdach (1776–1847), German Professor of Medicine,
looked beneath mental activity to a general property of all
living things, a plastic organizing principle like that of the
Christian Platonists. In 1829 he used the term "unconscious

formative life," and later wrote that "one should assume that the principle of life and of the mind are not different in essence, but only in their form of expression and stage of development."

Meantime the complement to this attempt to sweep everything tidily under one principle was expressed by E. A. Poe (1809–1848) in his *Imp of the Perverse:*

[On Perverseness]: In the sense I intend, it is, in fact, a *mobile* without motive, a motive not *motiviert.* Through its promptings we act without comprehensible object; or, if this be understood as a contradiction in terms, we may so far modify the proposition as to say, that through its promptings we act, for the reason that we should *not.* In theory no reason can be more unreasonable; but, in fact, there is none more strong.

Any objective "science of man" must curb itself so as to leave room for Poe's imp, and all the other paradoxical streaks in human nature.

C. G. Carus (1789–1869), German physician and another friend of Goethe, on whom he wrote a valuable interpretative study, is one of the most significant figures in our chain. He was a doctor and observer of men, with an attitude at once biological and religious. His strength and weakness are those of Goethe: he distrusts and perhaps does not appreciate the importance of the fine analysis of contrasts, and seeks to derive all phenomena, as it were deductively, from a central principle of life, dimly conceived as the *growth of forms.* Carus' root principle is unconscious and holistic. *"Alle Schöpfung ist Werk der Natur."* Though as a physician he cannot fail to recognize conflict and pathology, his emphasis is idealistic and optimistic, and he does not identify the peculiar frustrations of self-conscious man.

Carus' great work: *Psyche: Zur Entwickelungsgeschichte der Seele* (1846), is a landmark. Speaking as a physician, Carus claims that he is in possession of an important message for mankind: the recognition of the true nature of the unconscious mind. The opening sentence of this volume, which runs as a leitmotiv through its pages, reads: *"The key to the understanding of the character of the conscious life lies in the region of the unconscious."* (It is interesting that Freud's library, at his death, contained other works by Carus.) While the conflicts which were Freud's main concern were relatively neglected by Carus, these quotations show that Carus had a vivid sense of the importance of the sexual functions, unconscious as instinct and conscious as voluptuousness, in relation to the mind as a whole. His conception of the "subtle oscillations between unconscious and conscious" maintained through sexual relationships, describes something known to every sensitive observer.

Let us therefore above all assist ourselves by observing how many of the conscious states of our mind only develop and reach completion in an unconscious form.

From which it is clear that in willing, just as in knowing, the passage from the conscious to the unconscious is truly part of the highest human fulfillment.

Thus the possibility of the highest intensification of inner pleasure or delight lies in this region—for which language has a special word: voluptuousness—which is nothing other than the communication of the most intense and vital stimulation of the unconscious sphere of the sexual system to the highest conscious sphere of the nerves . . .

To emphasize that not merely in one case, but in many realms, the unconscious is the active principle of our mental life.

. . . [so we conclude that] one and the same kind of intelligence is effective in all these cases, and operates as a truly "unconscious thinking."

So gradually many other important distinctions between the conscious and the unconscious will become clear to us, for example, one becomes convinced that necessity rules throughout the realm of the unconscious, while freedom is based on the appearance of consciousness.

In the entire realm of unconscious mental life the conception of exhaustion does not apply.

This [sexual] desire, which in origin is necessarily an unconscious one, has the significance that, in all its excitations, it penetrates conscious and unconscious with equal force.

. . . so that the same subtle oscillation between unconscious and conscious, on which every truly human existence must rest, is also maintained right through this [sexual] relationship.

[Instinct, the prior form of human conscious life, is no special force, but] nothing other than an activity, like the simpler organic functions [breathing, digesting, etc.], but more complex and involving the entire organism, which is determined in the unconscious and is directed towards the requirements of the whole.

The unconscious is contrasted to the conscious, as the general is to the special. But the main difference is that the first flows continuously, while the second appears periodically.

The unconscious is itself the subjective term for what we objectively recognize as nature.

As I have said, Carus' penetrating interpretation of the unconscious mind was prejudiced by a somewhat sentimental idealistic and religious optimism, resulting in a neglect of conflict. A complementary and equally prejudiced view of the unconscious factors in history was expressed in the same year as Carus' book appeared (1846) by *K. Marx* (1818–1883) and *F. Engels* (1820–1895) in their materialistic and pessimistic doctrine of social conflict. Though they did not at that date employ the term "unconscious," they were keenly concerned with the material factors producing consciousness, the limited validity of conscious motives, the real interests concealed beneath ruling ideas, and so on. Their doctrine was, in fact, based on a philosophy of the collective unconscious of the social classes. (The index to the *Deutsche Ideologie* contains over 100 references under *Bewusstsein*.)

Since according to [the Young Hegelians'] fantasy, the relationships of men, all their doings, their chains, and their limitations are products of their consciousness, . . .

Morality, religion, metaphysics, all the rest of ideology and their corresponding form of consciousness, thus no longer retain the semblance of independence. . . . Life is not determined by consciousness, but consciousness by life.

Division of labor only becomes truly such from the moment when a division of material and mental labor appears. From this moment on consciousness *can* really flatter itself that it is something other than consciousness of existing practice . . . [and can] emancipate itself from the world and proceed to the formation of "pure" theory, theology, philosophy, ethics, etc.

It is quite immaterial what consciousness starts to do on its own.

The class which has the means of material production at its disposal, has control at the same time of the means of mental production. . . . The ruling ideas are nothing more than the ideal expression of the dominant material relationships.

During the nineteenth century there were many exact scientists who did not recognize the utility of the conception of "unconscious mental processes" and were inclined to assume that it was necessarily misleading.

For example, *O. Domrich,* German physiologist, wrote in 1848:

To postulate a special, mental, unconscious, lower central entity for these involuntary associative feelings and movements can only appeal to a philosopher who is not informed about the natural physiological relations of the organism.

But even in 1960 no one is yet so well informed as to be able to give a physiological description of mental processes.

VIII

The Discoverers:
1850–1880

In THE LIMITED PERSPECTIVE of the mid-twentieth century the history of our idea appears to start moving with a rush as it enters the 1850's. It would be possible to name some ten or twenty thinkers in each decade from 1850 to 1880 as having made minor contributions. Viewed more objectively it may be that in the hundred years from 1850 to 1950 only a very few, perhaps five, basic theoretical advances were made, mainly round 1900. Though the tempo seems to change after 1850, this is partly a matter of more professional workers in the field, and more thinkers either taking their own ideas too seriously or neglecting what had already been expressed. It was a time of increasing philosophical, biological, medical, and psychological specialization, and specialists—and above all teachers—cannot be expected to be continuously aware that their fundamental ideas may be old. In

retrospect it is both shocking and entertaining to observe
with what high seriousness each generation took its own
achievements, and how swiftly they were modified by the next.
What counts in the world of intellectual fashion is not novelty
or validity, but dramatic condensation, scholarly elaboration,
vivid presentation, and above all topical illustration and practical application. If one chose to look only for genuine intellectual originality, in the sense of historical priority of valid
formulations, much of the history of ideas would vanish from
sight.

Thus Carpenter's useful phrase "unconscious cerebration"
(1853)—to which we shall come in a moment—is either a cloak
for ignorance or a program for research; von Hartmann's stupendous *Philosophy of the Unconscious* (1868) added little,
except comprehensiveness, to Fichte, Schelling, Schopenhauer, Carus, and the others; Nietzsche's doctrine of vitality
and his clairvoyant poetry of the depths can be viewed today
as natural inferences from what had already been thought
and said for a hundred years.

Even those who enjoy flashes of intuition and are repelled
by laborious detailed research must recognize that *sub specie
aeternitatis* all this ancient wisdom began to acquire a new
power when workers such as Liébault, Charcot, and Bernheim took up the scientific study of hypnotism and hysteria.
That is why this study of the background ideas ends approxi-
mately at the time when their work began.

The work of the years 1850 to 1880 was mainly exploratory
and educative, a further move from the general speculative
and philosophical context of the earlier period toward the
subsequent quasi-scientific specialized methods of thought
and inquiry.

The birth of a relatively trivial term may mark a new
orientation in thought, and *W. B. Carpenter* (1813–1885),
English physician and naturalist, is now remembered for his

creation in 1853 of the term "unconscious cerebration." This had a strong appeal to physical scientists and physiologists, for it put the emphasis on an activity of the brain, and offered the promise of a monist interpretation, still to be discovered. It also appealed to many others, including philosophers such as J. S. Mill, and it entered common usage around 1870; Henry James wrote of the "unconscious cerebration of sleep" in his *Aspern Papers* (1888).

For Carpenter it was "a matter of no practical consequence, whether the doctrine be stated in terms of Metaphysics or of Physiology, in terms of *mind,* or in terms of *brain,* provided it be recognised as having a positive scientific basis."

That act of "unconscious cerebration," for so I call it, this unconscious operation of the brain in balancing for itself all these considerations, in putting all in order, so to speak, in working out the result—I believe that that process is far more likely to lead us to good and true results than any continual discussion and argumentation.

The mind has obviously worked more clearly and successfully in this automatic condition, when left entirely to itself, than when we have been cudgelling our brains, so to speak, to get the solution.

That action of the brain which, through unconscious cerebration, produces results which might never have been produced by thought.

A considerable part of Carpenter's *Principles of Mental Physiology* (1874) is devoted to a discussion of the evidence for unconscious cerebration, "an unconscious reflex action of the brain," or "process of Modification" of the brain, only the terminal results of which enter awareness. Chapter XIII of that book, entitled "Of Unconscious Cerebration," is in many

respects so up to date, so topical in its quotations on the working of the unconscious background of the imagination, and
so little known, that it might be taken as it is and offered to
a popular magazine in 1960.

In spite of the work of Maine de Biran, thinkers in France
paid little attention until c. 1870 to the conceptions of the
unconscious that were developing so rapidly elsewhere. It is
significant that the first known usage of *inconscient,* either
as adjective or noun, is in 1860 by a French-speaking Swiss, a
student of German literature and philosophy:

H. F. *Amiel* (1821–1888), in his famous *Journal:*

The dream is the reflection of the waves of the unconscious life
in the floor of the imagination.

9 August, 1862—Life, which seeks its own continuance, tends to
repair itself without our help. It mends its spiders' webs when
they have been torn; it re-establishes in us the conditions of
health, and itself heals the injuries inflicted upon it: it binds the
bandage again upon our eyes, brings back hope into our hearts,
breathes health once more into our organs, and regilds the dream
of our imagination. But for this, experience would have hopelessly
withered and faded long before the time, and youth would be
older than the centenarian. The wise part of us, then, is that
which is unconscious of itself; and what is most reasonable in
man are those elements in him which do not reason. Instinct,
nature, a divine and impersonal activity, heal in us the wounds
made by our own follies; the invisible *genius* of our life is never
tired of providing material for the prodigalities of the self. The
essential, maternal basis of our conscious life is therefore that
unconscious life which we perceive no more than the outer hemi-
sphere of the moon perceives the earth, while all the time indis-
solubly and eternally bound to it.

28 April, 1861—In the same way as a dream transforms, according to
its nature, the incidents of sleep, so the soul converts into psychi-

cal phenomena the ill-defined impressions of the organism. An uncomfortable attitude becomes nightmare; an atmosphere charged
with storm becomes moral torment. Not mechanically and by
direct causality; but imagination and conscience engender, according to their own nature, analogous effects; they translate into their
own language, and cast in their own mold, whatever reaches them
from outside. Thus dreams may be helpful to medicine and to
divination, and states of weather may stir up and set free within
the soul vague and hidden evils. The suggestions and solicitations
which act upon life come from outside, but life produces nothing
but itself after all. Originality consists in rapid and clear reaction
against these outside influences, in giving to them our individual
stamp. To think is to withdraw, as it were, into one's impression
—to make it clear to oneself, and then to put it forth in the shape
of a personal judgment. In this also consists self-deliverance, self-
enfranchisement, self-conquest. All that comes from outside as a
question to which we owe an answer—a pressure to be met by
counter-pressure, if we are to remain free and living agents. The
development of our unconscious nature follows the astronomical
laws of Ptolemy; everything in it is change—cycle, epicycle, and
metamorphosis.

Our greatest illusion is to believe that we are what we think ourselves to be.

Finally, here is Amiel's warning (very relevant today) to
those who would cast the impatient searchlight of conscious
attention on every seed of thought:

And if you feel something new, whether thought or sentiment,
awake in the root of your being, do not at all bring light or attention to bear on it quickly; protect the birth of the germ by forgetting it, surround it with peace, do not rob it of its darkness,
allow it to shape itself and to grow, and do not noise your fortune
abroad. Sacred work of nature, every conception should be en-
veloped in a triple veil of modesty, of silence, and of shadow.

Meantime in Germany the sequence of thinkers on the unconscious becomes so dense that selection is difficult, and well-known names must be neglected in order to leave room for a few of the forgotten.

I shall not, for example, quote from *H. Helmholtz* (1821–1894), though he is important for his emphasis on *unconscious inference*.

K. Fortlage (1806–1881), German philosopher and follower of Benecke, in his *System der Psychologie* (1855) stressed the basic importance of impulse and the association of unconscious processes with instinct, suggesting that only when they are repressed are special differentiated forms of instinct actually experienced, and that even then the primary undifferentiated instinct remains unconscious. Instinct itself, according to Fortlage, cannot make mistakes.

Consciousness is "a repressed instinct, or one arrested in its external effectiveness."

The act of perception perceives the rememberable content of an image, and this is itself unconscious.

Instinct is the most important part of the unconscious content of these images. It is the basis of consciousness. For consciousness is an arrested instinct.

It is not instinct as such which displays the characteristic of an imponderable, but only instinct in the uninhibited or unconscious condition. ["Imponderable" here means "like an imponderable or intangible physical fluid."]

These quotations show that Fortlage is concerned with a fundamental issue which was relatively neglected by Freud: *the general conditions which evoke awareness.* Freudian theory is mainly concerned with a less general problem: the conditions generating a *pathological loss of awareness,* after it has developed.

I. H. Fichte (1796–1879), psychologist, son of the philosopher, is also concerned with the development of awareness as a mode of response.

Beneath *active* consciousness there must lie consciousness in a merely potential state, that is a middle condition of the mind, which though not yet conscious, nonetheless positively carries the specific character of Intelligence; from those conditions of preconscious existence the true consciousness must be explained and developed step by step.

One must therefore first distinguish an unconscious and a conscious region in the life of the mind, which are nonetheless intimately interconnected in such a manner that what enters conscious presentations only develops itself from the flowing depths of dark feelings and activities and sinks back into them again. This unconscious, but rich and indeed inexhaustible background always accompanies our clearly conscious mental life, which in comparison is relatively meager. But we can learn of the depth of its range, and what hidden treasures it contains, when we turn our attention to these phenomena of dreams, of insight, and so on.

Thus the first genesis of consciousness can only be the product of a reaction, the response of our still unconscious mental life to an external stimulus. Left to itself, innerly closed against relations with anything other, even for the nature of the mind there would be no cause for change, and it would thus be incapable of reaching the condition of awareness.

Consciousness as such is not productive, brings forth nothing new.

In 1858 *G. H. Lindner's* important *Lehrbuch der empirischen Psychologie nach genetischer Methode* appeared, in which Herbart's psychology, including his theory of the conflict of ideas on the threshold of awareness, was treated as the most reliable approach to the understanding of the mind from an empirical and developmental point of view.

G. T. Fechner (1801–1887), German psychologist, exerted great influence (he was much admired and closely followed by Freud) through his contributions to psychophysics, his work on the threshold of consciousness—he compared the mind to an iceberg mainly below the surface and moved by hidden currents as well as by the winds of awareness—and by his conceptions of mental energy, of a topography of the mind, his pleasure-unpleasure principle, and his principle of constancy (universal tendency toward a stable regular form).

W. M. Wundt (1832–1920), German physiologist, developed Fechner's ideas between 1860 and 1880, and held that we become conscious of our activities mainly through resistance and conflict, that is, through their frustration. Our proper activity is unconscious. He was keenly interested in unconscious creative synthesis:

Our mind is so fortunately equipped, that it brings us the most important bases for our thoughts without our having the least knowledge of this work of elaboration. Only the results of it become conscious. This unconscious mind is for us like an unknown being who creates and produces for us, and finally throws the ripe fruits in our lap.

As further evidence of German professional attention to unconscious mental activities in the 1860's, here is the influential physician-psychologist *W. Griesinger* (1817–1868), in his book *Mental Pathology and Therapeutics* (taken from the English translation, 1867):

There is in intelligence an actual, though to us an unconscious, life and movement; we recognise it however by its results, which often suddenly make their appearance from some unexpected source. A constant activity reigns over this almost, if not wholly, darkened sphere, which is much greater and more characteristic for the individuality than the relatively small number of impressions which pass into the state of consciousness.

This appreciation of the unconscious formative imagination from German experimental physiology (not from physiological *theory*, which is silent on such matters) makes a convenient transition to a Scottish critic of art, *E. S. Dallas* (1828–1879). These quotations are taken from his *Gay Science* (1866), a study in the theory of art criticism.

The "imagination" is a name given to the automatic function of the mind or any of its faculties—to what may not unfitly be called the Hidden Soul.

Outside consciousness there rolls a vast tide of life which is perhaps more important to us than the little isle of our thoughts which lies within our ken. . . . Each is necessary to the other. . . . Between our unconscious and our conscious existence, there is a free and a constant, but unobserved traffic for ever carried on.

The mind is an organic whole, and lives in every part, even though we know it not.

The spectator brings to the art object a total experience far deeper than he could consciously fathom.

[The Hidden Soul never reasoned, abstracted, or dissected;] it worked through metaphor, comparing wholes with wholes, seeking from art parallels to its own latent intuitions.

Meantime in Britain a school of physicians had been quietly developing a doctrine of unconscious mental activities as part of their professional task of trying to understand the patient as a body-mind unity. To these pragmatic monists there was nothing strange or challenging in the idea of unconscious factors; whether one chose to call them physiological or mental, they were indubitably at work. We have already seen that Sir William Hamilton had taken up the German ideas, and that W. B. Carpenter had followed him. They were succeeded by many, of whom the most important are perhaps J. D. Morell, J. C. Brodie, H. Maudsley, T. Laycock, and D. H. Tuke.

Morell suggested in his *Elements of Physiology* that a line cannot be drawn between the organic and the psychical forces, and that it is only by a mental fiction that we distinguish the conscious processes so sharply from the unconscious. In 1860 Laycock wrote:

No general fact is so well established by the experience of mankind or so universally accepted as a guide in the affairs of life, as that of unconscious life and action.

Vital successional states and conscious successional states are due to a common law, a law of design which includes both.

Maudsley summarized the ideas of this English school of thought in his *Physiology and Pathology of the Mind* (1867), where he wrote:

The most important part of mental action, the essential process on which thinking depends, is unconscious mental activity.

This leads on, after 1880, to William James, and to F. H. W. Myers' "subliminal self."

It is interesting to note that in 1874, the year Freud entered the University, Brentano published in Vienna a detailed examination of Maudsley's views, and that Freud attended Brentano's lectures for two years.

It is not surprising that a German metaphysician (this is not a pejorative term, for "an unconscious metaphysic moulds every life") considered that the time had come to make the Unconscious the central principle of a philosophical system.

E. v. Hartmann (1842–1906) presented in his massive *Philosophy of the Unconscious* (1868) a comprehensive survey of German philosophy and of Western science, interpreted in the light of one principle, partly "transcendental" and partly "empirical," of unconscious mental process. Von Hartmann's work and its influence throughout Europe has sometimes been underestimated.

By 1882 this book had gone into nine editions in Germany; it was translated into French in 1877 and into English in 1884, and was extensively reviewed in all three countries. For example, the French reviews around 1870 display awareness of the fact that unconscious mental activities had been widely discussed throughout Europe, but most of all in Germany, during the previous decades. Von Hartmann had struck at a favorable moment; the unconscious was in the air; and alarm was even being expressed in some quarters at the threat it presented to established ideals and principles, for that was already clear to some.

It is true that the power of the new idea to disturb and transform Western ways was then only evident to a few. Our quotations represent the advanced intuitions of searching minds and the vast bulk of the science and literature of the schools did not recognize the long-term significance of the movement.

Yet this must not be misunderstood. Around 1870 the "unconscious" was not merely topical for professionals, it was already fashionable talk for those who wished to display their culture. The German writer, von Spielhagen, in a period novel written about 1890, describes the atmosphere in a salon in Berlin in the 1870's, when two topics dominated the conversation: Wagner and von Hartmann, the music and the philosophy of the unconscious, Tristan and instinct.

As often happens in the history of thought, an idea may be fashionable and even transform society before it is properly understood. The atomic nucleus was discovered in 1911; it is now transforming human life; but it is not yet understood in the sense that gravity, crystal structure, and chemical actions already are. The unconscious mind, in the post-Cartesian sense, was discovered around 1700; it is now transforming Western thought; who would dare to claim that its basic laws are yet understood? Freud did not.

Von Hartmann's *Philosophy of the Unconscious* is a vast enterprise—the English 1931 translation fills 1100 pages—covering in its fashion nearly all conceivable aspects. The chapter headings refer to twenty-six topics, from neural physiology, movements, reflexes, will, instinct, idea, curative processes, plastic energy, sexual love, feeling, morality, language, mysticism, history, metaphysics, ultimate principles, and even *the use of probability theory to justify the inference of mental causes from material events*. Von Hartmann surveys his predecessors, giving a discussion of the ideas of the Vedas, Leibniz, Hume, Kant, Fichte, Hamann, Herder, Schelling, Schubert, Richter, Hegel, Schopenhauer, Herbart, Fechner, Carus, Wundt, and several others. He does not, however, indicate what several have noticed, that his work is an expansion of the ideas of Carus' *Psyche* into a comprehensive metaphysical and quasi-scientific system. Carus had already digested much earlier thought, and had transformed it into an intuitive picture of the nature of man; von Hartmann broke it up again, went back to all the sources and claimed to be re-presenting it as a systematic philosophy. His work is an extraordinary achievement in 1868, and it proves that when Freud was twelve years of age, twenty-six aspects of unconscious mental activity in man had already been considered in detail in a famous work. But it is neither good philosophy nor good science. It does not state what is known and what is not known; what are the real problems; how they should be solved; or what effect their solution might have on man.

How can one quote from 1100 pages, which are partly echoes of earlier writers, partly a Hegelian whirl of words, and partly descriptions of scientific facts? Here are a few passages, chosen at random, to show that von Hartmann could see far in 1868:

The principle of practical philosophy is to MAKE THE ENDS OF THE UNCONSCIOUS ENDS OF OUR OWN CONSCIOUS-NESS. [His capitals.]

Female chastity alone protects social relations from complete disorder.

The bee . . . without ever having seen the life, carries in itself the unconscious representation of the hexagonal cell, accurate to half an angular minute.

The *vis medicatrix* [unconscious reparative power of nature].

. . . we must recognize a clairvoyance of the unconscious in the purposiveness of the creative impulse as in that of instinct . . .

Such quotations could be endless. Everything seems to be there, but without the clear discriminations of science and the concentration on important unknowns that marks genius. There could not be a greater contrast between von Hartmann, the verbalizing philosopher digesting everything, and Freud, the seeker after special truths to be used for a clear purpose. Yet for the student of the history of ideas von Hartmann's book, and the response it received in many countries, is proof that by 1870 Europe was ready to discard the Cartesian view of mind as awareness, but not prepared to wait any longer for physiology to take over the problem. Nor was Freud himself: around 1890, confronted by neurotic patients, he began to drop his neurophysiology and sought to develop a psychological interpretation of neurosis. Fortunately he had not read von Hartmann. He may have been unconsciously influenced in his general attitude by Schopenhauer, Nietzsche, and Dostoevsky—for even if he personally read little of these writers in his early years, they were being widely read in Vienna in the last two decades of the century. Yet in their recognition of the unconscious depths of the mind, these three great writers were in no sense original, they were merely presenting once again, in new images and in a new context, what had long been known to a few. They are original in their own dimension, but not in the history of the human mind.

In one sense no writer ever was more without precedent in his material or method than Dostoevsky, and his penetrating insight into unusual states of mind has never been surpassed. Yet the immense response to his novels shows that the orientation of his thought must correspond closely to a widespread experience in our time. And on analysis we find that many of the aspects of deep psychology with which he was concerned were those that were being actively explored by philosophers, physicians, and psychologists throughout the nineteenth century. One may call these aspects *the pathology of consciousness,* first explicitly studied in the previous century, and taken up in the nineteenth for professional investigation in particular realms: hysteria, epilepsy, the paralysis of spontaneity through unconscious conflict of motives, the anticipatory and curative significance of dreams, and so on. Dostoevsky was, like every other fertile genius, a man of his time, bringing an old tradition of ideas to new life by reliving it in his own passionate experience. Here the personal and the universal are fused. Dostoevsky seems to be describing freak pathology; but he is illustrating at the same time less-recognized levels of the normal. Some of his most striking characters are so riddled with contradictions that we can scarcely accept them—but what about ourselves? To take an extreme example: Dostoevsky seems to be excessively concerned with the quality of a man's consciousness when he believes that death is near—but is this so irrelevant as we may consciously suppose?

Just because Dostoevsky is so deeply aware of contradiction and complexity, and not an impatient theorizer, his vivid sense of the harmonies and cacophonies of the unconscious cannot properly be illustrated by quotations. I will content myself with one passage from *The Idiot* (1868), referring to a dream:

These obvious absurdities and impossibilities with which your dream was overflowing . . . you accepted all at once, almost without the slightest surprise, at the very time when, on another side, your reason was at its highest tension and showed extraordinary power, cunning, sagacity and logic. And why, too, on waking and fully returning to reality, do you feel almost every time, and sometimes with extraordinary intensity, that you have left something unexplained behind with the dream, and at the same time you feel that interwoven with these absurdities some thought lies hidden, and a thought that is real, something belonging to your actual life, something that exists and always has existed in your heart. It's as though something new, prophetic, that you were awaiting, has been told you in your dream.

This survey of leading opinion from 1850 to 1880 makes it all the more striking that Freud's work was treated with angry professional scorn from 1905–1915, as stupid as the same profession's blind adulation which followed swiftly, from 1935–1945. Why were Freud's doctrine and methods found so despicable—a matter for official taboos and police action—if the background had been so long prepared and he was to be recognized as a major figure a generation later?

The answer is perhaps that Freud's explicit and narrow emphasis on sexuality · as the source of neurosis disturbed many who were not ready—as Freud was—to admit into theory and clinical practice what they had inhibited—as Freud also had—in their own lives. Freud mercilessly exposed their lesions; more than that he claimed to be doing it in the name of science and enlightenment, though sexuality is only one aspect of the vital *élan* in man. To be exposed is bad enough; to have that done to one in the name of a harmonizing principle would perhaps have made it tolerable. But to be told that sexual conflict was the cause of all neuroses and that the fear of incest lay at the bottom of everything, this was hateful and Freud was duly hated—until he himself (from 1920 onward) and later many of his followers, unconsciously took "Freud" *cum grano salis,* knowing well that sexuality is only one expression, inseparable from all the others, of the organic tendencies in man. But there was no assurance of that when Freud began his incisive analysis and self-analysis from 1890 to 1900, nor indeed up to 1920.

Around 1870–1880 the story passes out of our scope. This means that such names as Charcot, Bernheim, Delboeuf, Lotze, Bertrand, Lipps, Janet, Breuer, Galton, Tuke, Morton Prince, James, Myers, Hudson, Lombroso—all of whom made contributions before 1899 when Freud's *Interpretation of Dreams* was published—can only be mentioned. Nor can we consider the work of those who since 1900 have, either independently or in some degree following Freud, developed these ideas further (Weininger, Havelock Ellis, Jung, Adler, Rank, and many others) or applied them in philosophy (Bergson) or literature (Proust, and many writers of this century).

I have given sufficient evidence to show that the general conception of unconscious mental processes was *conceivable* (in post-Cartesian Europe) around 1700, *topical* around 1800, and *fashionable* around 1870–1880. Also that many special applications of the idea had been systematically developed from 1800 onward. My object in doing this is in no degree to belittle Freud's achievement, which would be absurd, but to show that an immense background of sustained thought by a large number of individuals in many countries unconsciously or semiconsciously influences and supports even the most original of minds. As is well known, Freud explained that he avoided reading Schopenhauer and Nietzsche until late in life, "I was less concerned with priority than with preserving my impartiality," just as Boyle, the chemist, said that he had avoided the Democritean and Cartesian doctrines for fear of prejudicing his inferences from experiment. In a letter to Fliess, written on August 31, 1898, Freud shows some disappointment at discovering that Theodor Lipps had expressed some of his own basic assumptions in a work published in 1883. This shows that when Freud was forty-two he was unaware that at least fifty writers (probably many more) had been developing similar assumptions for over two hundred years.

Finally in 1925, at the age of sixty-nine, Freud wrote: "The overwhelming majority of philosophers regard as mental only the phenomena of consciousness. For them the world of consciousness coincides with the sphere of what is mental." This curious mistake shows how narrow his reading had been, and how wrong a conception he must then have had of his own originality. The inference is that not only Freud but *most of us are largely unaware of what has made us what we are and led us to think as we do, and it is sometimes as well that we should be ignorant.*

In any case it cannot be disputed that by 1870–1880 the general conception of the unconscious mind was a European commonplace, and that many special applications of this gen-

eral idea had been vigorously discussed for several decades.
Nor was this interest restricted to narrow circles, for:

1. The circulation of works such as von Hartmann's suggests that at least fifty thousand Europeans paid some attention to these ideas during this decade.

2. During the same decade at least six other books were published with the word "unconscious" (or its equivalent in German or French) in the title, showing that publishers were ready to seize the opportunity resulting from this widespread interest:

1872, W. B. Carpenter, *Unconscious Action of the Brain;*

1872, J. C. Fischer, *Hartmann's Philosophie des Unbewussten. Ein Schmerzenschrei des gesunden Menschenverstandes;*

1873, J. Volkelt, *Das Unbewusste und der Pessimismus;*

1877, C. F. Flemming, *Zur Klärung des Begriffs der unbewussten Seelen-Thätigkeit;*

1877; A. Schmidt, *Die naturwissenschaftlichen Grundlagen der Philosophie des Unbewussten;*

1880, E. Colsenet, *La Vie Inconsciente de l'Esprit.*

3. Even in France where the idea seems to have met more resistance than in Germany or England, it became topical at this time. For example, during the six years, 1872–1877, three lengthy surveys [13] of contemporary thought on the unconscious mind were published by Renouvier, Janet, and Dumond—the last citing fourteen German authors from Kant onward.

4. In the 1870's three writers independently developed theories of *unconscious organic memory:* Eduard Hering, Thomas Laycock, and Samuel Butler.

I shall close this historical survey by referring to five writers, each remarkable in her or his own way, whose names might not be found in the index of any narrower professional survey, but who showed around 1870 a keen awareness of the importance of the unconscious levels of the mind: an English-woman of wide interests, an American poet and essayist, a French poet, a French historian, and finally one of the most penetrating minds ever to have used the German language. None of these, I believe, had anything new to say, but they expressed old truths in a new context, and to a new audience.

I have found no woman writer since Descartes (that excludes Santa Teresa) who put on record her interest in the unconscious mind earlier than the intelligent *Miss Frances Power Cobbe,* who contributed regularly to English monthlies between 1860 and 1880. She was certainly a wide reader, and she reflects advanced opinion in England fourteen years before the first translation of von Hartmann appeared in London. *Macmillan's Magazine* for November, 1870, contains an excellent review article by her on "Unconscious Cerebration" mentioning Leibniz, Hamilton, and Carpenter, among others, and giving a lucid summary of the mental faculties which, on the basis of her reading and personal experience, she credited to the "Unconscious Brain." In this she found nothing alien to her Christian faith.

Four months earlier the American anatomist, essayist, and poet, *Oliver Wendell Holmes,* had been reading a paper to the Phi Beta Kappa Society at Harvard on "Mechanism in Thought and Morals," which included the following wonderful passage:

The more we examine the mechanism of thought, the more we shall see that the automatic, unconscious action of the mind enters largely into all its processes. Our definite ideas are stepping-stones: how we get from one to the other, we do not know: something carries us; we do not take the step. A creating and informing spirit which is with us, and not of us, is recognized everywhere in real and in storied life. It is the Zeus that kindled the rage of Achilles: it is the Muse of Homer; it is the Daimon of Socrates; it is the inspiration of the seer; it is the mocking devil that whispers

to Margaret as she kneels at the altar; and the hobgoblin that cried,
"Sell him, sell him!" in the ear of John Bunyan; it shaped the
forms that filled the soul of Michael Angelo when he saw the
figure of the great Lawgiver in the yet unhewn marble, and the
dome of the world's yet unbuilt basilica against the blank horizon;
it comes to the least of us, as a voice that will be heard; it tells us
what we must believe; it frames our sentences; it lends a sudden
gleam of sense or eloquence to the dullest of us all, so that, like
Katterfelto with his hair on end, we wonder at ourselves, or rather
not at ourselves, but at this divine visitor, who chooses our brain
as his dwelling-place, and invests our naked thought with the
purple of the kings of speech or song.

After all, the mystery of unconscious mental action is exempli-
fied, as I have said, in every act of mental association. What happens when one idea brings up another? Some internal movement,
of which we are wholly unconscious, and which we only know by
its effect. What is this action, which in Dame Quickly agglutinates
contiguous circumstances by their surfaces; in men of wit and fancy,
connects remote ideas by partial resemblances; in men of imagination, by the vital identity which underlies phenomenal diversity;
in the man of science, groups the objects of thought in sequences
of maximal resemblance? Not one of them can answer. There is
Delphi and a Pytoness in every human breast.

[Katterfelto was a German quack and conjurer who was the rage
in London from 1782 to 1784.]

On May 15, 1871, the poet *Arthur Rimbaud* (1854–1891)
wrote in *Lettre du Voyant:*

For *I* is someone else. If the upper vessel awakes as a clarion, it's
not in the least its fault. This is quite clear to me: I assist at the
unfolding of my thought: I watch it. I listen to it: I make a stroke
of the bow: the symphony stirs in the depths, or comes on the
scené at a leap.

If the old imbeciles hadn't only discovered the wrong meaning of ME, we wouldn't have had to clear away the millions of skeletons who, for infinite ages, have been piling up the products of their intelligences fit only for a one-eyed old woman, while crying out that they are authors.

In Greece, as I said, poetry and the lyre provide the rhythm of action. Later, music and rhyme become games, relaxations. The study of the past charms the inquisitive; several pleased themselves by renewing antiquity—that's for them. The universal intelligence has always sent forth its ideas naturally; men collect a part of these fruits of the brain; then act on them, and use them to write books; that's how the advance went on, man not working, indeed not yet being awake, or not yet as fully awake as he was lost in the great sleep. Officials, writers. The Author, the creator, the poet: this man has never existed! The first study for the man who wants to be a poet is to know himself; he looks for his mind, inspects it, tries it, learns it. When he knows it, he must cultivate it! That seems simple: in each brain a natural development works itself out; so many *egoists* claim to be authors: many others take credit themselves for their intellectual progress! . . . I say that one must be a seer (*voyant*), make oneself a *seer*.

The following passages from *H. A. Taine* (1828–1893) French historian and critic, show that many of the ideas we have been considering were by 1870 circulating there almost as freely as in Germany. They are taken from his essay *Sur l'Intelligence:*

We get a glance here at the obscure and infinite world extending beneath our distinct sensations. These are compounds and wholes. For their elements to be perceptible to consciousness, it is necessary for them to be added together, and so to acquire a certain bulk, and to occupy a certain time; if their group does not attain this bulk and does not last this time, we observe no change in our state. Nevertheless, though it escapes us, there is one; our internal sight has limits; outside these limits, internal events, though real, are for us as though they did not exist. They gain accession, they undergo diminutions, they combine, they are decomposed, without our being conscious of it. They may even, as we have just seen in the case of sensations of sound, have different degrees of recoil, beyond the grasp of consciousness. The elementary sensations directly making up our ordinary sensations are themselves compounded of sensations of less intensity and duration, and so on. Thus, there is going on within us a subterranean process of infinite extent, its products alone are known to us, and are only known to us in the mass. As to elements and their elements, consciousness does not attain to them, reasoning concludes that they exist; they are to sensations what secondary molecules and primitive atoms are to bodies; we have but an abstract conception of them, and what represents them to us is not an image, but a notation.

But, besides the mental events perceptible to consciousness, the molecular movements of the nervous centers also arouse mental events imperceptible to consciousness. These are far more numerous than the others, and of the world which makes up our being, we only perceive the highest points, the lighted-up peaks of a continent whose lower levels remain in the shade. Beneath ordinary sensations are their components, that is to say the elementary sensations which must be combined into groups to reach our consciousness. By the side of ordinary images and ideas are their collaterals, I mean the latent images and ideas, which must take their turn of preponderance and ascendancy in order to reach consciousness.

Having settled this, we see the moral world extending far beyond the limits assigned to it. We are accustomed to limit it to events of which we have consciousness; but it is now plain that the capacity of appearing to consciousness belongs only to certain of these events; the majority of them do not possess it. Outside a little luminous circle lies a large ring of twilight, and beyond this an indefinite night; but the events of this twilight and this night are as real as those within the luminous circle . . .

One can therefore compare the mind of a man to a theater of indefinite depth whose apron is very narrow but whose stage becomes larger away from the apron. On this lighted apron there is room for one actor only. He enters, gestures for a moment, and leaves; another arrives, then another, and so on. . . . Among the scenery and on the far-off backstage there are multitudes of obscure forms whom a summons can bring onto the stage or even before the lights of the apron, and unknown evolutions take place incessantly among this crowd of actors of every kind to furnish the stars who pass before our eyes one by one, as in a magic lantern.

Finally here are some passages from an intuitive who expressed old insights with extreme clarity: *F. Nietzsche* (1844–1900). It was not surprising that he saw so much, for his passionate temperament sought to replace Christianity by a doctrine of vital energy as the source of everything, natural, human, and divine. Nietzsche never had any doubt that the conscious mind is the instrument of unconscious vitality, and he invented the term "Id" (for the impersonal elements in the psyche subject to natural law), which Freud took over at Groddeck's suggestion. The following are taken, almost at random, from works written between 1876 and 1888:

Where are the new doctors of the soul?

Consciousness is the last and latest development of the organic, and is consequently the most unfinished and least powerful of these developments.

The absurd overvaluation of consciousness.

The awakening consciousness is a danger; and whoever lives among conscious Europeans knows in fact that it is an illness.

Every extension of knowledge arises from making conscious the unconscious.

Our consciousness limps along afterward.

Consciousness only touches the surface.

The great basic activity is unconscious.

For it is *narrow,* this room of human consciousness.

Every sequence in consciousness is completely atomistic.

The real continuous process takes place *below* our consciousness: the series and sequence of feelings, thoughts, and so on, are symptoms of this underlying process.

The conjecture that consciousness in general developed itself only under the pressure of the need to communicate.

We flatter ourselves that the controlling or highest principle is in our consciousness.

"I did that," says my memory. "I could not have done that," says my pride, and remains inexorable. Eventually the memory yields.

All our conscious motives are superficial phenomena: behind them stands the conflict of our instincts and conditions.

IX

The Prospect

It WOULD BE SUPEREROGATION for me to attempt a summary of Freud's ideas; that has already been done from many points of view. But I wish to say something of the significance of his work, as a link between this survey of pre-Freudian ideas and the present chapter which seeks to look ahead.

As we have seen, Freud's supreme achievement was to force the attention of the Western world to the fact that the unconscious mind is of importance in every one of us, by giving dramatic illustrations of the way in which it works, particularly when its spontaneous formative processes are deformed by inhibition. He was the first systematically to connect the general idea with a wide range of particular distortions of behavior in a way that is manifestly valid to unprejudiced minds. Freud changed, perhaps irrevocably, man's image of himself. Beside this it is of secondary import that some of his valid ideas were not new, his special conceptions questionable, and his therapeutic methods uncertain. One side of his nature sometimes doubted the apparent conviction of another side: that understanding by an individual of the genesis of his neurosis must of itself ensure a cure.

Freud's extraordinary influence on the English-speaking world is probably due—as already suggested—to two factors: his own profound sense of a mission, and the fact that his doctrine, by making man fully aware (by inference) of his unconscious, offered the conscious person a chance of recovering—some day—a more natural relation to the universal. For Freud no such true recovery was conceivable; man was cursed forever with the separation, even if only partial, of Superego, Ego, and Id—for "the character of being foreign to the Ego" defines the Id. Inhibition, for him, necessarily led to essential deformation, frustration, and pathology. Civilization and psychopathology were one. However, his vast audience, who accepted the unconscious but not the structure he imposed on it, dimly perceived in his lifework the promise of something better: the overcoming of pathology in a genuine relation of the individual to the organic. The Western world has acclaimed Freud as a great emancipator, because it sensed that he opened the path through and beyond Freudian ideas to a more natural, more organic, and more humane condition.

Freud was not the first person to identify himself with the mission of enlightening man by revealing to him his own unconscious mind. In a pale manner Carus experienced this task as a mission of redemption. But for Freud the mission gained in intensity from its tragic limitation. Man was doomed to frustration; let him at least know the truth about himself. "Where Id is, there Ego shall be." He did not say: where conflict is, there unconscious organic coordination shall be.

This message of doom dignified by scientific clarity met two great needs of the early twentieth century: apparent scientific reliability, and a myth of human experience as we know

it, which means for many conflict, fission, and disorder. Freud
is here an exemplar of our time, though his puritanical
moralism and narrow conception of scientific method mark
him personally as pre-Freudian, what we sometimes call
"Victorian." He was the last pre-Freudian rationalist, pas-
sionately upholding a rationalism of the conscious intellect
which his doctrines would rapidly undermine. As was once
said to me, "Freud didn't really believe in the unconscious";
he did not actually like it, or libido, or the free imagination.
For, as his biographer has told us, he spent most of his life
afraid of his own free fancy, and sought security in a stern
moralism, a naïve rationalism, an exact materialistic physiology, and a psychology based on the attempt to eliminate
complexity. In this a true Cartesian, his spirit sought rest
and assurance in experimental physiology and exact science.
Though Freud had read Goethe extensively, his revolt from
him and from *Naturphilosophie* to exact science expressed
his overpowering need for the kind of mental security that
analytical thinking seems to promise.

Freud's strength in his early period lay in his self-limitation
to the analytical study of conflict in its extreme pathological
expressions. He was not seriously interested in the universal,
the historical, and the normal. He neglected not only philosophy, but also the historical approach to the present condition of man, and behind these lay an even more surprising
and enlightening limitation: the lack of an adequate recognition of the primary fact of the organic and human realms:
the pervasive order and coordination in all organisms, though
in his later years he paid it lip service. Sexuality, which he
enjoyed little in his own experience though it is the source
of beauty in most human lives, took its revenge by obsessing
his thinking *to the exclusion of the biological order which
sexuality serves, and to which it is normally subordinate.*

This is intended to be understood *sub specie aeternitatis;*

it is no criticism of a specialist genius born in 1856 that he failed to recognize an issue which is only coming to the forefront in the late twentieth century. For I assert the following: *Freudian and Neo-Freudian psychological conceptions will only be replaced by a more reliable and comprehensive theory of the human mind after exact science has established a valid theory of biological organization.* The "unity of the mind" resides in a biological coordination of its differentiated aspects. Whether the future scientific understanding of this biological unity comes from a physical biology, a biological physics, or from a neutral structural theory of complex systems, does not concern us here. But it is unlikely that the human mind can comprehend its own states of coordination merely by attention to its awareness, or even by inferences therefrom, without the aid of guiding principles of organic order gained from the objective study of organisms. Freud was the genius of conflict in the psyche; he should be followed by the genius of order in the organism illustrated in the human mind. Freud asked, "What is the origin and nature of psychic conflict?" The next question is: "What is *not-*conflict? What is the source and character of organic coordination?"

Ernest Jones wrote [14] that "a good deal of [Freud's] more theoretical expositions were, *as he would certainly have agreed,* responses to his own intellectual needs, rather than assertions of general validity. *As he said himself,* they were scaffoldings he found useful, but which could be replaced at any time if better ones were found." (My italics.) If Freud and his followers had maintained this wise caution all the time, the movement would have been less subject to criticism, and the world would have been spared vain polemics. For the detailed study of psychic conflict may be one of the best routes toward a general theory of psychic order and disorder.

Freud's limitations, as person or thinker, were perhaps inevitable; they were certainly fertile. But the limitations of the profession are less excusable. I repeat: the uncritical adulation of Freud by one school from 1935 to 1945 was as stupid as the scorn of an earlier one from 1905 to 1915.

In 1913, when opposition to Freud was at its height, Henri Bergson [15] recognized the importance of the new science of depth psychology:

To explore the most sacred depths of the unconscious, to labor on what I have just called the subsoil of consciousness, that will be the principal task of psychology in the century which is opening. I do not doubt that wonderful discoveries await it there, as important perhaps as have been in the preceding centuries the discoveries of the physical and natural sciences.

Knowledge advances in waves, and the forty years which have passed since Freud's most fertile period have added little that is both new and objectively valid to the science. The "depths" still remain obscure.

This judgment implies no failure to recognize Jung's work as an intuitive reinterpreter of ancient knowledge, or the contributions of Adler, Rank, and others at work in this field during the last three decades. Freud's pseudo-scientific sharpness was his strength and weakness; the complementing breadth of later workers is necessary, but remains vague. Some may even doubt whether a valid psychological theory can be analytically sharp, since the biological, and even more, the human realm is distinguished by its complexity and variety. The issue is still open: *What operations of the human brain-mind admit exact analysis?* Many techniques are converging toward an answer.

But this answer may not imply "a scientific theory of the human mind" applicable to any individual situation as a classical physical theory was to a classical physical system. It is likely that the relation of theory to particular facts must change as knowledge moves into realms where the pervasive interactions cannot be neglected. The isolated object is already losing its autonomy in current physics, for its frame of reference is nothing less than the entire universe, and this tendency may go further. It is the task of any new theory in the psychic realm to achieve both sharpness and balance, if necessary by a new limitation of its scope.

This study leads to the following conclusions regarding the contributions of two past periods to the understanding of the human mind:

1680–1880: Widespread discovery of the *existence* of the unconscious mind, in the context of post-Cartesian thought.

1880–1960: Partially successful attempts to uncover the *structure* of unconscious mental processes, at first mainly in pathology.

To this I add a guess as to what lies ahead:

From 1960: More attention to *undeformed* mental processes and their monistic interpretation, with less emphasis on the antithesis conscious/unconscious, within the context of a developing theory of biological organization.

There are indications that the antithesis conscious/unconscious may have exhausted its utility. The "unconscious" may already have passed its climax. From 1920 onward Freud saw the most important classification elsewhere, in the contrast between uninhibited thought flowing to fantasy fulfillment and thought deformed by inhibitions finding expression in the real world. Hence his pessimism: all "real" life, in his experience and his theory, is deformed.

But there are other signs, not dependent on Freudian conceptions:

Conscious and unconscious aspects are now recognized not to be on a par: the first being transitory, discontinuous, and self-eliminating; the second continuous, and self-developing.

It is not the separation of two realms but their unification as aspects of one complex continuous activity which is now held to be primary.

It is unsatisfactory to define the more general by a negative: *un*conscious. The next task is to identify the general characteristics of those mental processes which are now designated as "not directly given in awareness."

The irrelevance of these two concepts to fundamental principles is also suggested by the fact that the basic biological function and structural meaning of both terms are still obscure, after many generations of quasi-scientific usage.

That the self cannot doubt that it is aware appeared lucid and self-evident to Descartes. But what is the "self" and what is "awareness"? Several of the philosophical schools that sprang from Descartes have ended in what appears to be an impasse.

When Wittgenstein wrote in 1922: "The world is everything that is the case," he evoked the whole problematic of human existence, and that may be too much for the intellect to digest along the path of logical analysis of the meaning of the meaning of words. An alternative is to pay attention at the start to the fact that knowledge arises within a complex human context: the largely unconscious mental processes of the imaginative social organism *Homo sapiens*. This is certainly a difficult path to follow, but there may be no other way. Since the early seventeenth century the situation of the Western intellect has changed. Then, as Descartes said, the prime need was to make a fresh start by choosing simple clear ideas for what seemed to be self-evident facts. This succeeded so well, that as then understood it may now be exhausted. In mid-twentieth century nothing is simple or self-evident, for we have become aware of the web of complexity of which all existence is part. Our need today is not for simplicity, clarity, or certainty here and now; we have learned that that is too much to ask. Things are complex, and what the mind needs to find is *some order* in the complexity, the mind itself being an ordering organ which even imposes a spurious order when necessary as a short cut or a first step. Instead of immediate clarity and certainty we need something both less and more: a provisional working hypothesis concerning the kind of order in each complexity. Less, because tentative; more, because admitting complexity at the start.

The conception of "order" is highly general, but nonetheless it can be made fertile. In certain fields it has already been given clear meanings and this challenges us to discover its appropriate meaning in others. The kind of order in most chemical molecules, in crystals, and in the solar system is known; that in atomic nuclei, in living systems, and in brain-minds is not. Temporal succession illustrates one type of order; regular spatial patterns another. Moreover, any one kind of order may be combined with aspects of disorder in ways we do not understand. Finally, the two great tendencies apparent in the universe: toward order and toward disorder, seem to be locked in a cosmic opposition, perhaps because we view them wrongly. We do not yet know (outside certain special fields) when or how order subdues disorder. And within this universal warfare there are here and there human brain-minds impatiently reducing everything to order.

But *what* is the brain-mind ordering all the time? The best answer available today is: *contrasts*. We perceive internal or external contrasts, differences, and distinctions, and we infer that they are contrasts between "one thing" and "another"; the logicians class these contrasts as "relations." The attention of an animal with a brain is always directed (when the animal is attentive) to some contrast, and human awareness is the "impressing" of a "trace" representing some contrast on the "dominant processes" of the central nervous system in man. However, these assertions clarify little; they are merely the enunciation of a program of research: to make evident what it means to say that *thought is the dominant ordering process in an animal with a brain-mind.* If physiology is to contribute a solution, it will probably not be based on classical atomic mechanics, or relativistic mechanics, or quantum mechanics, but on a science which will not be mechanics in a traditional sense: a general theory of order and disorder in complex systems. Here we enter the realm of unknowns which we are slowly learning to formulate as questions.

But even the posing of questions presupposes some language. How to avoid a false start? A. B. Johnston [16] gave a hint when he wrote (1836), "We make language the expositor of nature, instead of making nature the expositor of language." I have sought to allow the facts to clarify words, and the least prejudicial starting point that I have discovered is the following:

This is a
UNIVERSE OF CONTRASTS
grouped into
COMPLEXES OF RELATIONS
with aspects of
ORDER AND DISORDER
including
CHANGE AND TENDENCY

We begin with some *group of contrasts* separable from the totality. This appears to have the logical character of a complex system of relations (between things, if you will). Such groups may reveal a temporal order, interpreted as the changes of a system of things, and in certain cases as a tendency toward some apparent terminus. The stress is on *complex systems of changing relations displaying tendencies toward order or disorder,* not on simple unchanging entities. For intellectual convenience or for other reasons, it may be necessary *to infer an invisible world of immutables:* of gods never directly known, or of one or more classes of persisting atomic particles, to account for the stability of the world of appearances. These issues are not prejudiced by the present argument.

In this context of a universe of contrasts displaying the temporal and logical character of changing complexes of relations with tendencies toward order or disorder, the crucial issue in any particular situation is:

What forms of order and disorder and what tendencies can be identified in any given complex of relations?

This is the general question characteristic of our time, which allows us to pass to its applications to special questions now confronting any theory of the human mind:

1. *The problem of life:* What contrasted forms of order distinguish animate and inanimate phenomena? What is the nature of biological organization and its relation to physical laws, either known or still to be discovered? How sharp is the boundary?

    It would seem that until a general theory of (or method of approach to) order and disorder in complex systems of various kinds has been established, theoretical science cannot come to grips with the "problem of life," since this appears to involve ordered transformations in complex systems. Current theories of protein and nucleic acid structure, etc., provide no suggestions of how differentiated processes are coordinated spatially and temporally within living systems.

2. *The general problem of "mind":* What is the structure characteristic of "mental processes"? What aspects of these enter direct awareness? How should types of awareness be classified?

It may be possible to identify, within the wider class of organic processes, a category of mental processes which can either be observed externally as physiological phenomena, or known subjectively. "Mental" may be defined (as in Chapter II) as referring to those "dominant ordering processes in which traces of individual experience are ordered and tend to order thought and behavior." But this is ambiguous, since the meaning and uniqueness of "dominance" has still to be determined.

If "finality" (the property of proceeding toward a terminus) is accepted as a characteristic of mental processes, and if mind is taken to be part of nature, then the general laws which determine the processes of the mind must themselves be finalistic.

3. *The problem of man:* Wherein is man unique? In what respects, if at all, does he escape the restrictive conditions of all other organisms? Are any universally valid biological principles irrelevant to man? How far do the contrasted methods of the various sciences apply to man?

Most centuries have had their own answers to these or similar questions. Certainly biology is not in a position to claim finality for any current answers. *Homo* may be distinguished by his use of tools, mastery of fire, or size of brain; *Homo sapiens* perhaps by his ability to draw, to speak, to write, to read, or to think *step-by-step* about one thing at a time. For our own species seems to be marked by the cerebral faculty to form *new commu-*

nicable units of thought. But here we are still ignorant, and surprises are likely.

4. *The problem of human consciousness:* What is the role of human "awareness" and "self-awareness" and which mental processes are necessarily unconscious?

These questions have been considered in Chapter II.

5. *The problem of "reason":* Has the term "reason" a useful meaning today? If so, what is its relation to other mental faculties?

It is not easy to give this term a single, acceptable meaning. To call reason "the guiding principle of the human mind" merely conceals our ignorance as to what this principle is. "Logical reasoning" would restrict it to the highly specialized operations of deductive logic and calculation. "The ordering process of the human brain-mind" might be a useful interpretation, but this process is largely unconscious.

6. *The problem of disorder in the human mind:* If man is an organic species, and the brain-mind a differentiated organ, why have human thought and behavior lost the perfect coordination of structures and functions which prevails in organisms that survive?

The easy answer is: he lost it through the Original Sin (or some genetic misfortune), and he will *not* survive.

Another is: man passed through a historical discontinuity and thus acquired freedom of choice; he has thereby moved outside the biological realm of organic order. But this cannot be the correct answer since animals continually select between alternatives without frustrating hesitation, damaging conflict, or permanent disorder.

Another possible answer is that man's fifty thousand years or more as a stabilized species have not been enough; that he is a *not-yet-adapted* species: that he still has to complete the exploitation of his hereditary species potentialities in an adequate social tradition ordering both thought within the individual, and individuals within the race; and that a mature characteristically human organic-social order lies ahead, if he can survive the transitional lack of adaptation.

This is a dreamy hypothesis of an ultimate stationary adaptation. But it has been suggested that the most rapid known evolution of a new adapted animal species has required about half a million years, certainly much more than *Homo sapiens* has yet had. And if our species can already explore cosmic time and space with its instruments why worry if it possibly needs a mere thousand generations or so more to realize its organic potentialities, mentally and socially? For this is the only human ideal that can be universally accepted forever: the full realization of the biological potentialities characteristic of the species, subject to any minor eugenic modifications.

7. *The problem of the "depths" of the human mind:* What is the meaning of "depth" psychology? How far is the human psyche an autonomous part of the human system, with obscure "abysses" of its own?

The term "depth" psychology confuses the issue by combining two contrasted meanings: *hidden far from direct awareness,* and therefore accessible only by difficult procedures; and *concerned with highly general tendencies* underlying all differentiated and all conscious activities. The second meaning can be combined with a physiological conception of highly general traces involved in all the dominant processes of the brain, and affecting all special activities. Subjectively "deeper" tendencies might then correspond to "higher" tendencies in the nervous hierarchy.

Topographical theories of the mind, assuming its approximate division into higher, middle, and lower regions, may have exhausted their value. At one point it seemed as if Freud and Jung were approaching the "depths" of the mind by complementary paths, Freud from personal experience toward biological instinct, and Jung toward historical-social forms. But each influenced the other; the topographical scheme is ambiguous and ultimately misleading; and behind both approaches lies an aim recognized by both Freud and Jung in their later work: to identify an objective organic foundation at the root of the mind.

Many alternative views are possible. No one has yet clarified and coordinated all that is implicit in the original work of this century in the realm of depth psychology.[17] We are not slaves who are compelled to choose between Freud and Jung; we can take what is valid from both if we can create a true fusion. But this may require new principles.

8. *The problem of personal coordination:* In spite of the prevalence of clash, and of the still inescapable disorder in the human mind and tradition, can each person at times experience in himself the harmonious cooperation of the differentiated functions and faculties? Can each person directly experience the fact and the operation of "organic coordination"?

I believe that this experience is not merely possible, but frequent: in joy in living, when self-awareness is replaced by aesthetic participation. Without this positive core life would be unbearable.

Three Historical Charts

A. Changes in Intellectual Awareness in Post-
Medieval Western Europe (c. 1300 onward)

B. The Transition from Static toward Process
Concepts (1750 onward)

C. The Successive Discovery of Three Aspects
of the Unconscious Mind

N.B. These charts simplify highly complex historical facts.

CHART A

CHANGES IN THE DOMINANT INTELLECTUAL AWARENESS IN POST-MEDIEVAL EUROPE (c. 1300 ONWARD) BETWEEN

FOCUSED SELF-AWARENESS, ANALYTICAL METHODS, AND STATIC CONCEPTS

&

1500

1600 A developing self-awareness expressed in a new term: "self-conscious." Analytical methods, quantities, and relatively static concepts are treated as primary.

1700 STATIC ABSTRACT RATIONALISM
The partial and abstract character of this outlook provokes a

⎣————————————————————————————————→

1800

1900 Prestige of rational analytical intellect is prejudiced by the absence of any clear fundamental concept or principle of *transformation*.
No theory available of conditions under which static concepts are valid, or of true function of *awareness*, or *self-awareness*.

A Broader, Potentially Unifying, Sense of Process as Primary

The underlying sense of process is not yet expressed in nonreligious language. As medieval thought loses its authority (c. 1300 onward) the individual acquires

Historical outlook gradually develops. Unconscious mind *conceivable* (c. 1700).
New emphasis on the immediacy and primacy of change. Transition toward process concepts begins (c. 1750).

REVOLT FROM STATIC REASON.
Nature viewed as process.
Unconscious mind *topical* (c. 1800).
Unconscious mind *fashionable* (c. 1870).

No monistic philosophy or science of transformation yet in sight.

CHART B

THE TRANSITION FROM STATIC TOWARD PROCESS CONCEPTS (1750 ONWARD)

Names are set in italic, or in boldface, according as their basic relevant concepts *did not*, or *did*, involve the idea of temporal succession. Exclamation marks denote thinkers in this respect contrary to the "dominant" mode (1750 taken as transition).

Period of Static Concepts

	History (of solar system, earth, and human societies)	Philosophy Psychology	Biology	Physics
1600	**BACON!**			*GALILEO, KEPLER*
	DESCARTES! (Cosmogony, history)	*DESCARTES* (Metaphysics)	*HARVEY, DESCARTES* (Machine-Organism)	*DESCARTES* (Mathematical theory)
		SPINOZA		
1650	**British geologists! FONTENELLE!**	**LEIBNIZ!**	(Study of stable organic forms and cycles)	*NEWTON*
1700	(From 1700 onward developmental ideas spread from historical and geological studies toward the special sciences.)			
	VICO! MONTESQUIEU! VOLTAIRE!	*BERKELEY*	*LINNAEUS*	

1750 **LESSING**	**ROUSSEAU**	**BUFFON, MAUPERTUIS, DIDEROT, WOLFF, LA METTRIE, E. DARWIN, LAMARCK**	
HUME, KANT, CONDORCET, GIBBON, HERDER	**HUME, KANT, HAMANN, HERDER, GOETHE**		
1800 **HEGEL**	**HEGEL, SCHELLING, SCHOPENHAUER**		**CLAUSIUS** and **KELVIN** introduce statistical, non-fundamental concept of entropy
1850 **MARX**	**MARX**	**C. DARWIN, WALLACE**	*MAXWELL !*
	NIETZSCHE		*EINSTEIN !*
1900	**FREUD, BERGSON, JUNG**		*Quantum Mechanics !*
	RUSSELL !		
TOYNBEE !			
1950			

CHART C

THE SUCCESSIVE DISCOVERY OF THE COGNITIVE, VITAL, AND PATHOLOGICAL ASPECTS OF THE UNCONSCIOUS MIND IN POST-CARTESIAN EUROPE

N.B. Four aspects have been so widely recognized, or are so subtly connected, that they fall outside this historical analysis: 1. the *Mystical* (from earliest times to Kierkegaard); 2. *Memory*; 3. *Dreams*; and 4. the *Collective* (from Vico to Jung). What is here called the Vital Unconscious, properly understood, should include the others as its varied expressions.

COGNITIVE	VITAL	PATHOLOGICAL
(Apperceptions, perceptions, images, ideas)	(Instinct, will, motives, emotions, imagination)	
	Paracelsus (1493–1541)	
	Montaigne (1544–1592)	
	Shakespeare (1546–1616)	
	Pascal 1623–1662) and	
	Spinoza (1632–1677), all show a background awareness	
From c. 1680		
CUDWORTH		
NORRIS		
MALEBRANCHE	(Shaftesbury)	
LEIBNIZ		
VICO		
v. WOLFF		
KAMES		

1650

1700

1750	CRUSIUS CONDILLAC TUCKER KANT	(Rousseau)	
	1800 FICHTE	HERDER LICHTENBERG FICHTE, GOETHE SCHELLING The Romantics TROXLER HERBART MAINE DE BIRAN SCHOPENHAUER	from c. 1780 HERDER MESMER MORITZ REIL LANGERMANN BERTRAND HERBART
	HERBART MAINE DE BIRAN		
	1850 HAMILTON MARX – ENGELS CARPENTER	HAMILTON CARUS FORTLAGE DOSTOEVSKY AMIEL VON HARTMANN	SCHOPENHAUER BENECKE MORELL, GRIESINGER LAYCOCK, MAUDSLEY CHARCOT, BRENTANO BERNHEIM, JANET BREUER, LIPPS
	GALTON		
1900	JUNG	FREUD JUNG	FREUD JUNG

Notes

1. L. L. Whyte, *Listener* (London: British Broadcasting Company), Vol. 52, July 15, 1954, 91.
2. W. Windelband, *Die Hypothese des Unbewussten* (Heidelberg: Akad. d. Wissenschaften, 1914).
3. A. B. Johnson, *Treatise on Language* (1836), Univ. California Press, 1947 (Lecture 24, ¶ 8).
4. For 16 distinct usages of "unconscious" see: J. G. Miller, *Unconsciousness* (London: Chapman & Hall, 1942). Mine corresponds to Miller's usage 16: ₄ "Unaware of discriminating; unavailable to awareness."
5. B. L. Whorf, "Time, Space, and Language" in L. Thompson, *Culture in Crisis* (New York: Harper, 1954). Also B. L. Whorf and J. B. Carroll, *Language, Thought, and Reality* (London: Chapman & Hall, 1956), p. 80.
6. P. Radin, *Primitive Man as Philosopher* (New York: Dover; London: Mayflower & Vision Press, 1957), p. xxi.
7. D. Hume, *Treatise of Human Nature*. Of Morals, Part 3, Section 3.
8. D. Diderot, *D'Alembert's Dream,* tr. Birrell (London: Routledge, 1927).

9. A. O. Lovejoy, *The Revolt against Dualism* (London: Allen & Unwin, 1930).

10. E. L. Margetts, "Concept of the Unconscious in the History of Medical Psychology," *Psychiatric Quarterly*, 27 (1953), 1.

11. J. Vyvyan, *The Shakespearean Ethic* (London: Chatto & Windus, 1959), p. 161.

12. On the content of this paragraph see E. L. Margetts, "Historical Notes on Psycho-somatic Medicine," in *Recent Developments in Psycho-somatic Medicine*, Wittkower and Cleghorn, eds. (London: Pitman, 1954).

13. L. Dumont, *Revue Scientifique* (December 28, 1872); C. B. Renouvier, *La Critique Philosophique*, I (1874), 19, 231, 293, 386; P. Janet, *Revue des Deux Mondes* (June 1, 1877).

14. E. Jones, Prefatory Note to Issue on Freud, *British Journal for the Philosophy of Science, VII* (1956), 1.

15. H. Bergson, *The Independent* (New York, October 30, 1913).

16. A. B. Johnson, *Treatise on Language* (1836), Univ. of California Press, 1947, p. 59.

17. An attempt in this direction has been made by I. Progoff in *Death and Rebirth of Psychology* (New York: Julian, 1956).

References

To most quotations in Chapters V–VIII, in same sequence as in text.

(Except where indicated, the translations are those of the author, L. L. Whyte.)

CHAPTER V

GALEN, in Siebeck, *Geschichte der Psychologie*, 1880–1884 (p. 195).

PLOTINUS, in Siebeck, *Geschichte der Psychologie* (p. 338).

AUGUSTINE, *Confessions*. Tr. Sheed (London: Sheed and Ward, 1943) (Book 10, ¶ 8).

AQUINAS, Philosoph. Texts. Tr. Gilbey (London: Oxford University Press, 1951) No. 292.

ECKHART, Tr. Blakney. 1941 (p. 50).

DANTE, *Purgatorio*. Tr. Money (Canto 33).

PARACELSUS, *Paracelsica* by C. G. Jung (p. 94).

JOHN OF THE CROSS, *Dark Night of the Soul* (Ch. XII).

MONTAIGNE, *Essays*. Tr. Reeves, Turner. 1902 (Vol. II, Ch. 6).

DESCARTES, *Oeuvres*. 1908 (Vol. 10, pp. 180/188). Also Adam's *Vie* in Vol. 12. See also M. LEROY, *Descartes, le Philosophe en*

Masque, 1927. J. CHEVALIER, *Descartes* (p. 41). J. MARITAIN, *Le Rêve de Descartes*.

PASCAL, *Thoughts*. 1888 (pp. 77, 103, 307/8).

H. MORE, *Immortality of the Soul* (III. Ch. 12).

J. MILTON, *Paradise Lost* (Book V. ll. 100–121).

J. DRYDEN, *Works*. Ed. Scott-Sainsbury. II (pp. 129–130).

R. CUDWORTH, *True Intellectual System of the Universe*. 1678 (I. p. 346).

J. NORRIS, *Practical Discourses (Cursory Reflections)*.

N. MALEBRANCHE, *De la Recherche de la Vérité*. 1675 (I. p. 413).

SHAFTESBURY (A. A. COOPER, Third Earl), *Exercises (Philosoph. Regimen. On the Natural Self)*.

G. KEITH, *The Magick of Quakerism*. 1707.

G. B. VICO, *The New Science*. Tr. Bergin, Fisch (Ithaca: Cornell University Press, 1948).

C. v. WOLFF, See Grau, *loc. cit.* (Bibliography) (pp. 182–196).

KAMES (HENRY HOME, LORD K.), *Essays on the Principles of Morality*. . . . 1751 (p. 260).

CHAPTER VI

C. A. CRUSIUS, see Grau, *loc. cit.* (Bibliography).

J. J. ROUSSEAU, *Rêveries d'un Promeneur* (4th, 6th). *Confessions*. 1947 (pp. 419–20).

J. G. HAMANN, *Schriften*.

E. YOUNG, *Conjectures on Original Composition*. 1759.

D. HARTLEY, *Observations on Man*.

A. TUCKER, *Light of Nature Pursued*. 1768 (Vol. I, Pt. I, Chs. 5, 10).

D. HUME, *Treatise of Human Nature* (Book 2, Part 3, Section 3).

G. C. LICHTENBERG, *Deutsche National Literatur* (Vol. 141, pp. 47–89).

D. SIMPSON, *Discourse on Dreams and Night Visions*. 1791.

I. KANT, *Anthropology* (I. § 5).

E. PLATNER, *Philosophische Aphorismen*. 1776.

H. G. v. HERDER, *Vom Erkennen und Empfinden. Werke*. 1876 (Vol. 17, pp. 178–211).

C. P. MORITZ, Ed. Magazin zur Erfahrungsseelenkunde (1783–1793).

J. G. FICHTE, Grundlage der gesammten Wissenschaftslehre. 1794 (p. 374). 1802 (p. 161). Science of Rights. 1889 (p. 497).

NOVALIS (F. v. HARDENBURG), Schriften, Kluckhohn, ed. (Vols. II, III).

J. G. CABANIS, Rapports. 1799 (pp. 312–313).

J. C. REIL, Entwickelung einer allgemeinen Pathologie. 1815 Vol. III. p. 220).

J. G. E. MAAS, Versuch ueber die Einbildungskraft. 1792.

F. J. W. v. SCHELLING, Werke (I. Vol. 3, p. 612). Sämtl. Werke. 1858 (I. p. 348).

J. W. v. GOETHE, Last quotation is from Letters (transl. Herzfeld, Sym. 1957). See also Gespräche 2 (234); Schr. d. Goethegesell. 21. (122, 203) 1827.

J. C. F. v. SCHILLER, Briefwechsel mit Körner. 1847. (I, p. 381).

CHAPTER VII

J. P. F. RICHTER (JEAN PAUL), Sämtl. Werke. 1841 (Vol. 18, p. 60). Selina (p. 165).

W. WORDSWORTH, Prelude.

S. T. COLERIDGE, Statesman's Manual (App. B). Letters I (377). Biographica Literaria II (120).

G. H. v. SCHUBERT, Ansichten von der Nachtseite der Naturwissenschaften. 1805 (pp. 197/8). Lehrbuch der Menschen- und Seelenkunde. 1883 (p. 145).

M. DE BIRAN, Oeuvres inédits. 1859. Essai sur les Fondements de la Psychologie. II. (pp. 12, 19). Des impressions affectives internes. V. (pp. 42, 46, 51, 203).

I. P. V. TROXLER, Blicke in das Wesen des Menschen. 1812 (p. 115).

G. W. F. HEGEL, Enc. d. Phil. Wiss. im Grundr. 1827 (p. 394).

A. SCHOPENHAUER, Welt als Wille (Vol. II, Ch. 32).

T. DE QUINCEY, Palimpsest of the Human Brain (p. 18).

A. J. F. BERTRAND, Du Magnétisme Animale. 1826 (p. 3). Traité du Somnambulisme. 1823 (p. 452).

J. F. HERBART, *Sämtl. Werke* (V. p. 19).

F. E. BENECKE, *Elements of Psychology*. 1871.

J. J. S. DE CARDAILLAC, *Études élém. de Philosophie* (2 vols. 1830).

C. NODIER, *Oeuvres*. V. (pp. 160, 161, 173, 188).

S. A. KIERKEGAARD, *Sickness unto Death*. (Pt. I).

SIR W. HAMILTON, *Lectures on Metaphysics*. 1859/60 (Vol. I. pp. 348/9).

K. F. BURDACH, *Anthropologie*. 1847 (p. 130).

E. A. POE, *Imp of the Perverse*.

C. G. CARUS, *Psyche*. 1846. *Vergl. Psychologie*. 1866 (p. 77).

K. MARX AND F. ENGELS, *Die Deutsche Ideologie*. 1845/6 (I: Feuerbach).

O. DOMRICH, *Die psychischen Zustände*. 1849 (p. 62).

CHAPTER VIII

W. CARPENTER, *Principles of Mental Physiology*. 1874.

H. F. AMIEL, *Journal*. 1889.

K. FORTLAGE, *System der Psychologie*. 1855.

I. H. FICHTE, *Zur Seelenfrage*. 1859 (pp. 20, 258). *Psychologie*. 1864 (pp. 8, 82).

W. M. WUNDT, *Beitr. z. Theorie der Sinneswahrnehmung*. 1862.

W. GRIESINGER, *Mental Pathology and Therapeutics*. 1867 (p. 27).

E. S. DALLAS, *Gay Science*. 1866 (I. pp. 194–207).

T. LAYCOCK, *Mind and Brain*. 1860.

H. MAUDSLEY, *Physiology and Pathology of the Mind*. 1867.

E. v. HARTMANN, *Philosophy of the Unconscious*. 1869. Trans. 1931.

F. DOSTOEVSKY, *The Idiot*. Tr. 1912 (p. 455).

F. P. COBBE, Essay on *Unconscious Cerebration* in *Darwinism and Morals*. 1872.

O. W. HOLMES, *Mechanism in Thought and Morals*. 1877.

A. RIMBAUD, *Lettre du Voyant*.

H. A. TAINE, *On Intelligence*. 1871 (pp. 115, 180, 278).

F. NIETZSCHE, For references see under *Bewusst* and *Bewusstsein* in *Nietzsche-Register* (Vol. XIX of *Werke*). See also *Bewusstsein und Organismus* (*Werke*, Vol. XIII, p. 239).

Bibliography

As stated in the text, no such survey can ever be complete. For example, E. T. W. Hoffman (1766-1822) and H. von Kleist (1777-1811) might have been included, but it was considered that German Romanticism was already sufficiently represented, as its interest in the unconscious is well known.

A. GENERAL

M. H. ABRAMS, *The Mirror and the Lamp: Romantic Theory and the Critical Tradition* (New York: Oxford, 1953).

A. BÉGUIN, *l'Âme romantique et le Rêve*. 2 vols (Marseille, 1937).

E. G. BORING, *History of Experimental Psychology* (2nd ed.; New York: Appleton, 1950).

F. M. CORNFORD, "The Unconscious Element in Literature and Philosophy," in F. M. Cornford, *The Unwritten Philosophy* (Cambridge University Press, 1950).

E. R. DODDS, *The Greeks and the Irrational* (Cambridge University Press, 1951).

K. J. GRAU, *Die Entwickelung des Bewusstseinsbegriffes im XVII und XVIII. Jahrhundert,* Erdmann. Abhandlungen zur Philosophie, Halle, Heft 39, 1916.

G. MURPHY, *Historical Introduction to Modern Psychology* (London: Hamish Hamilton, 1951).

H. SIEBECK, *Geschichte der Psychologie* (Gotha, 1880–1884).

G. ZILBOORG AND G. W. HENRY, *History of Medical Psychology* (London: Allen & Unwin, 1941).

B. SURVEYS OF THE HISTORY OF THE IDEA OF THE UNCONSCIOUS AND RELATED TOPICS

M. D. ALTSCHULE, *Roots of Modern Psychiatry,* including essay on "Growth of the Concept of Unconscious Cerebration," (New York: Grune, 1957).

D. BRINKMANN, *Probleme des Unbewussten* (Zurich: 1943).

M. DORER, *Historische Grundlagen der Psychoanalyse* (Leipzig: 1932).

H. ELLENBERGER, "The Unconscious before Freud," *Bulletin of the Menninger Clinic, 21* (1957), 3.

E. v. HARTMANN, *Philosophy of the Unconscious* (London: Kegan Paul, 1931).

F. KÜHLER, *Beiträge zum Problem des Unbewussten* 1936.

E. L. MARGETTS, "Concept of the Unconscious in the History of Medical Psychology," *Psychiatric Quarterly, 27* (1953), 115; "Historical Notes on Psycho-somatic Medicine," in *Recent Developments in Psycho-somatic Medicine,* Wittkower and Cleghorn, eds. (London: Pitman, 1954).

A. W. WATTS, "Asian Psychology and Modern Psychiatry," *American Journal of Psychoanalysis, 13* [25] (1953).

The essays by Margetts (1953) and Ellenberger (1957) are the best recent surveys by psychiatrists of the history of the idea of the unconscious. Margetts is more comprehensive, covering ancient India, Greece, and the Middle Ages, as well as recent Europe, whereas Ellenberger gives a careful interpretation, mainly since Leibniz. Their papers support and supplement my own studies, largely made before I found them. I wish to thank these authors for their assistance.

C. Studies of Freudian Doctrine, the Concept of the Unconscious, Etc.

E. Fromm, *Sigmund Freud's Mission* (London: Allen & Unwin, 1959).

S. Hook, ed., *Psychoanalysis and Scientific Method* (28 essays) (New York: N. Y. U., 1959).

E. Jones, *The Life and Work of Sigmund Freud,* 3 vols. (London: Hogarth, 1953-1957).

I. Levine, *The Unconscious* (1923).

A. C. McIntyre, *The Unconscious* (London: Routledge, 1958).

J. G. Miller, *Unconsciousness* (London: Chapman & Hall, 1942).

I. Progoff, *Death and Rebirth of Psychology* (New York: Julian, 1956).

P. Rieff, *Freud: the Mind of the Moralist* (London: Gollancz, 1960).

Additional bibliography, 1978 edition:

C. G. Jung *The Relations between the Ego and The Unconscious* (Collected Works, Vol. VII. London: Routledge & Kegan Paul, 1953)

D. Recent books and Essays

L. FREY-ROHR *From Freud to Jung: A Comparative Study of the Psychology of the Unconscious* (New York: Putnam, 1974)

A. KOESTLER *The Act of Creation* (London: Hutchinson, 1964)

R. B. ONIANS *The Origins of European Thought* (Cambridge University Press, 1968)

R. E. ORNSTEIN *The Psychology of Consciousness* (New York, Viking Press, 1972)

J. PIAGET The Affective Unconscious and the Cognitive Unconscious. *Journal of the American Psychoanlytical Association,* 21 (2) (1973)

A. STORR *The Dynamics of Creation* (London: Secker & Warburg, 1972)

P. E. VERNON (Editor) *Creativity,* (London: Penguin, 1970)

K. WILBER *The Spectrum of Consciousness* (Quest Book, 1977)

Name Index

Subject Index

A

adventure, the incomparable, 4
aesthetic awareness (*see* consciousness)
alternation of conscious and unconscious, 116, 124, 128 f., 144
in sexual activity, 149
anticipations, vii, viii
anxiety for precision, 19
assumptions and conclusions, ix
atomism, 94, 96
authors (egotistic), 173
awareness (*see* consciousness)

B

biology, *passim*, 9, 51, 64, 194–195
British contribution, 65, 103, 147, 161 f.

C

Cartesian dualism, 18, 26 f., 55 ff., 60 (*see also* Descartes)
Catholicism, 66, 104
caution, x, 157, 180
chastity, 165
China, 12, 25, 60, 64